The Young Profe

Pers~~onal~~
Finance

The Lifeplanner Series

There are many situations in life for which your education, your parents or your experience simply have not prepared you. In this major new series, Kogan Page and *The Daily Telegraph* have joined forces with a team of expert writers to provide practical, down-to-earth information and advice for anyone encountering such a situation for the first time.

The series addresses personal finance and consumer issues in a jargon-free, readable way, taking the fear out of planning your life. So whether you are thinking about buying a house, having a baby or just deciding what to spend your first pay cheque on, the Lifeplanner series will help you do so wisely.

Titles available are:

The Young Professional's Guide to Personal Finance
Your First Home – Buying and Renting

Forthcoming titles are:

Your Career and Your Family – Getting the Balance Right
Making the Most of Being a Student
Your First Investment Portfolio
Your Child's Education

Available from all good booksellers. For further information on the series, please contact:

Kogan Page
120 Pentonville Road
London
N1 9JN
Tel: 0171 278 0433
Fax: 0171 837 6348
e-mail: kpinfo@kogan-page.co.uk

The Daily Telegraph

The Young Professional's Guide to
Personal
Finance

Niki
Chesworth

**KOGAN
PAGE**

YOURS TO HAVE AND TO HOLD
BUT NOT TO COPY

First published in 1997

Kogan Page Limited
120 Pentonville Road
London N1 9JN

© Niki Chesworth, 1998

British Library Cataloguing in Publication Data

A CIP record for this book is available from the British Library.

ISBN 0 7494 1961 X

Typeset by JS Typesetting, Wellingborough, Northants.
Printed and bound in Great Britain by Clays Ltd, St Ives plc

Could you live off £62.45 a week?

Probably not, but that's current State pension for a single person and a reality facing many of today's pensioners who don't have their own pension. Will you be in that unhappy situation when you retire?

It doesn't look as if the State pension is likely to improve either. According to the Equal Opportunities Commission, the basic State pension in 1994 was 16% of national average earnings, but by 2030 it is forecast to be half that.

If you are among the millions not covered by a personal pension plan you need to seek advice fast. Even if you are in a company pension scheme it is estimated that only 1 in 100 people in a company pension scheme will retire on maximum benefits. *

Not only would a pension bring peace of mind but is it also the most tax efficient way of planning ahead as the Inland Revenue allows full tax relief on your pension contributions - 23% for a basic rate taxpayer and 40% for higher tax payers.

Bradford & Bingley is the largest financial institution on the high street to offer independent financial advice. Because they don't have their own pension and aren't tied to offering anybody else's they can help by giving impartial advice from amongst the best pension products on the market to find one that suits your demands and personal circumstances. The advice that they offer is completely free and without obligation.

* Source - Occupational Pensions. December 1992

DAILY TELEGRAPH LIFEPLANNER SERIES

The **Daily Telegraph Lifeplanner Series** is a major new series addressing personal finance and consumer issues for anyone encountering them for the first time. All provide practical, sensible advice and are written in an accessible, jargon-free style.

Your First Home

BUYING, RENTING, SELLING AND DECORATING

Niki Chesworth

Your First Home tackles the whole range of issues the first time buyer or tenant will encounter. It addresses contractual issues, maintenance, decorating, legal problems and much more to provide the reader with all they need when renting or buying their first home.

£8.99 Paperback 160 pages ISBN 0 7494 2529 6
Order ref: KT529   Published: November 1997

How to Manage Your Career, Family and Life

Cary Cooper and Suzan Lewis

How to Manage Your Career, Family and Life looks at the practical, financial and emotional problems faced by any dual-career couple or family. It tackles issues like working from home, childcare, house-keeping, spending time together and much more. Written by the UK's leading stress guru, this practical book will help you get your life on the right track and is essential reading for anyone trying to juggle a career, relationship, family and other ambitions.

£8.99 Paperback 160 pages ISBN 0 7494 2528 8
Order ref: KT528   Published: November 1997

The Young Professionals Guide to Personal Finance

Niki Chesworth

Consultancy fees are beyond the purses of young professionals, who have a practical attitude to finance and want to spend their money wisely. This book offers sound, impartial advice for their present situation and indicates the choices available.

Topics covered include:

A place to live in • Marriage and partnerships • life assurance and critical cover • Short-term savings • Long-term savings • Self-employment • Looking ahead • Where to get advice • Pension planning • Making a will.

£8.99 Paperback 160 pages ISBN 0 7494 1961 X
Order ref: KS961   Published: November 1997

These books are available from all good booksellers or direct from Kogan Page's Credit Card Hotline, telephone 0171 278 0545 or fax 0171 278 8198

EXPECTING THE UNEXPECTED

A "job for life" is a thing of the past and the Welfare State will only provide you with the flimsiest of safety nets in the future. We must all learn to be more entrepreneurial and self-reliant and the provision of a robust safety net is the key to your happiness and future peace of mind. **Nigel Farquharson Agencies Ltd (NFA)** has long foreseen this brave, new world and based its financial planning on a simple premise: always expect the unexpected!

NFA has the confidence in its own expertise to give **you** the confidence to face the financial future with equanimity – to know that whatever life throws at you, whether it is a golden opportunity or a rumbling dark cloud, you will have the resources to cope with a sure foot and an easy mind.

When you consult NFA, you are taking the first steps in drawing up a blueprint for a secure future: – a future born of confidence in yourself, confidence in your adviser and, above all, confidence in your financial ability to ride any storms. **NFA is the young professional's adviser for the entrepreneurial age!**

NEW DAILY TELEGRAPH GUIDES

Guide to Working for Yourself

Seventeenth Edition
Godfrey Golzen

"Virtually the standard work on the subject. Highly recommended"
THE GUARDIAN

An unrivalled guide to the problems likely to be faced in the first two years of self-employment, as well as a practical look at all aspects of going it alone. Among the topics covered are:

* legal requirements
* raising capital
* working from home
* keeping accounts and records
* self-assessed taxation and national insurance
* self-employment and its legal implications.

£9.99 Paperback 0 7494 2148 7 .
256 pages Published: March 1997

Guide to Working Abroad

20th Edition
Godfrey Golzen

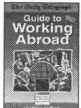

This best-selling guide to working abroad answers all your questions about finding work overseas as well as explaining the UK tax and welfare implications.

Part one – advises on children's education and home letting, discusses the problems of culture shock, and examines the potential in accepting an overseas contract.

Part two – surveys the 36 most popular destination countries across six continents. It gives details of local economies, tax systems, education, and living and working conditions, all drawn from expert and first-hand accounts.

£9.99 Paperback 0 7494 2395 1
320 pages Published: September 1997

Guide to Living Abroad

Tenth Edition

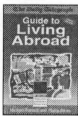

Michael Furnell and Philip Jones
This fully revised edition will arm you with all the essential facts you will need before moving abroad, as well as a wealth of information on the 22 destinations most popular with British expatriates. You'll find practical guidance on a wide range of facts including:

* moving overseas and settling in
* buying a property abroad
* tax, insurance and financial planning
* education and health matters
* returning to the UK.

£9.99 Paperback 0 7494 2385 4
320 pages Published: May 1997

Guide to Lump Sum Investment

Ninth Edition
Liz Walkington
This comprehensive and practical guide answers all your questions on the various short and long-term lump sum investment possibilities. Topics covered include:

* fixed capital investments
* gifts and equities
* unit trusts and offshore funds
* investment trusts and PEPs
* pension planning
* where to go for advice.

£9.99 Paperback 0 7494 2399 4
374 pages Published: June 1997

Guide to Taking Up a Franchise

Twelfth Edition
Colin Barrow and Godfrey Golzen
"recommended for anyone considering a franchise" Business Finance

£9.99 Paperback 0 7494 1836 2 • 272 pages 1996

How to Set Up and Run Your Own Business

Twelfth Edition
"A book full of sensible advice to those entering business for the first time."
Franchise Magazine
£9.99 Paperback 0 7494 1969 5 • 240 pages 1996

These books are available from all good booksellers or direct from Kogan Page's Credit Card Hotline, telephone 0171 278 0545 or fax 0171 278 8198

Contents

Introduction

Money: we argue over it, worry about it, and when we are not earning it we are spending it. Yet few find time to make the most of it.

As a young professional you are likely to spend 100,000 hours earning during your working life and can expect to be paid upwards of £2 million. Even though you may be struggling financially today in the future you will probably manage to buy two or three homes, invest for a rainy day, build up a pension and – by the time you retire – become reasonably wealthy.

The last things you may want to think about while you are climbing up the career ladder may be losing your job, saving for the future or the distant prospect of retirement. But failure to manage your finances, to take out insurance, and to pick the right mortgage, pension and investments could cost you dearly. If you make the wrong financial decisions, you could find that when you come to retire in the year 2030 or 2040 you are £100,000 or £200,000 poorer than a colleague who has earned the same salary.

If that seems too distant a scenario to worry about today, this might concentrate your mind: by managing your finances you could easily be £1000 or £2000 better off this year. If you were swindled out of that sum of money think how you would feel. Remember, the only person you are robbing is yourself.

This book is aimed at young professionals – people with potentially high earnings who spend so much time working that they have little time to make their money work. As you will probably be new to the world of personal finance, it is written with the minimum of jargon and the maximum amount of practical advice.

But this will be of little use if you fail to act. And the sooner you act the better.

Wealth Warning: Every effort has been made to ensure the accuracy of advice and information contained in this book. However, finance is a highly technical subject and the topics covered in this book are subject to change. Readers are advised to seek professional advice before making any investment decision.

1 Managing Your Money

A fool and his money are easily parted.

First you have to change the way you think about money. It is all too easy, after spending hours working hard to earn it, to waste it. You will probably need to set aside a quiet weekend to sort out your finances. But you should find that this is time well spent.

Step One: The Draft Budget

You must first find out where your money goes. Start by keeping a log of your day-to-day expenditure for a month. Then go through the past three months' to a year's pay slips, bank statements, credit card bills, household bills, receipts and other financial documents so you can work out your expenditure more accurately. Only after you have worked out where your money goes each month can you work out where savings can be made and how much money you have spare to save and invest. It will help concentrate your mind if you pay particular attention to the bills that you hate paying, such as bank charges and overdraft fees (many of which can easily be avoided).

On a blank sheet of paper write your monthly income on the left-hand side and on the right your expenditure. In addition to major bills, such as rent or your mortgage repayments, include all other expenditure: household bills, council tax, insurance, travelling costs, shopping, video rentals, TV licence, newspapers, books, CDs, records, average monthly clothes expenditure, dry-cleaning bills, the average you spend on going out, lunches and other expenses at work, and any other incidentals. Be as accurate as you can.

Then deduct your expenditure from your income to find out how much you have spare to save and invest or, more likely, how much you are spending in excess of your income.

Remember this budget does not include items of capital expenditure such as furniture, kitchen equipment, decorating, or emergencies such as a new engine for the car.

Step Two: Controlling Spending

Work out how much of this expenditure is unnecessary. As a busy, young professional the chances are that many of the following will apply to you:

▪ fines at the video shop because you are too busy to take the video back

▪ expensive shopping bills at the corner shop because you are too tired or do not make time to go to the supermarket

▪ several taxis a week because you do not have time to walk/take a train, bus or tube

▪ bank charges incurred because you did not know you were about to exceed your overdraft limit or because you did not make time to arrange a facility with your bank

▪ paying over-the-odds for things like insurance because you do not bother to shop around

You may feel that it is necessary for you to buy expensive clothes for work, to go out for lunch with colleagues to help your career, and to pay extra for day-to-day household expenses because you will gain in the long run by spending more time at work.

However, consider this. If you spend an average of £7 on a take-away twice a week, over a year you will spend over £700. By limiting this treat to once a week you would save over £350. Just by thinking twice before spending you should be able to cut your outgoings by up to 10 per cent.

Make a note of where you can cut your expenditure. Be realistic. After all, there is no point in working hard if you cannot enjoy the fruits of your labour.

Then work out ways to cut your expenditure on essential items. These are bills that you cannot avoid or cut out of your budget such as for gas, electricity and telephone. However, just because these bills cannot be avoided does not mean they cannot be cut. If you think you can make a saving act as soon as possible. A delay will reduce the savings you can make and once you put things off until to tomorrow there is a tendency to forget them forever.

How to cut your insurance premiums, mortgage repayments, bank charges, and credit card and loan interest is covered later in this book.

Look at ways to cut your telephone bills (sign up for BT discounts or switch to a cable company), your fuel bills (ask your local electricity company for energy saving tips) and even your council tax (you can appeal if a physical change to your neighbourhood has affected the value of your property).

ARENA

THE ORIGINAL MAGAZINE FOR MEN

£ CASH TIP £

If you are sent an estimated bill, check your meter reading. If you are not paying enough you could be in for a shock. If you are asked to pay too much, remember you can make better use of your money than allowing a utility to sit on it!

£ CASH TIP £

Pay by direct debit, that way you cannot forget to pay a bill and you can spread the costs. And you qualify for discounts of up to 4 per cent. However if your direct debit means you are paying too much ask for it to be cut. You do not want your utility company to owe you money.

Step Three: The Revised Budget

Now that you have worked out areas of unnecessary expenditure and have looked at ways to cut your regular bills, it is time to revise your monthly budget. Recalculate your outgoings so that you either have spare cash at the end of the month or at least are not getting further into debt.

Once you have drawn up a revised budget, stick to it.

Step Four: Setting Goals

As an incentive to keep within your budget you should set yourself targets. These may be cutting your overdraft, saving up for a deposit on a new house/a new car, or simply making sure you have enough set aside to protect you should you lose your job. You should set short-term goals as well as longer term ones so that you are rewarded more quickly for the efforts you have just made.

Short term goals:

- cutting monthly spending by £100

- reducing overdraft by £200 a month

- saving £50 a month

- switching borrowings to cheaper rates

Medium term goals:

- paying off your overdraft

- saving up a deposit for a flat/house

Long term goals:

- investing enough so that you can retire at fifty

- being financially secure so you no longer have to worry about money

- building up a lump sum so you can start your own business

Step Five: Organizing Your Finances

Now organize your finances. Set up a filing system so that you always know where to find the warranty when the dishwasher breaks down, can check how much you paid on insurance last year to see if your premiums have soared, and never need to waste time scrabbling around to find a bill or receipt.

One of the easier ways to organize your finances, particularly if you are computer literate, is by using your PC. There are several stand-alone software programs that allow you to organize accounts at home. You can use a budgeting spreadsheet to plan ahead.

Once you have your system in place you should only have to spend an hour or two each month checking that your bills are paid, that your bills are accurate and that you are meeting – or ideally exceeding – your goals.

Can *you find a* **better value** *index-tracking* PEP?

NO *initial charge*
NO *withdrawal fee*
0.5% *annual management charge*

The UK Index-Tracking PEP from
Legal & General is linked to the performance
of the FTSE All-Share Index, so if Britain's
companies do well, you will too.
Call free today and see how
index-tracking could work for you.

Lines open 8AM – 8PM weekdays, 9AM – 5PM weekends

0500 11 66 22

Please quote reference number B4GY01 when you call

**Legal &
General**

Call free now. Or to receive a free Legal & General pen please return the reply card at the back.

2 Banking

Look after the pennies and the pounds will look after themselves.

If you can make your current account work for you rather than you work to service your bank and interest charges, you will not only be richer but will also find managing your money less stressful. You could easily be spending several hundred pounds a year in unnecessary bank and interest charges if you regularly exceed your overdraft limits.

More than nine in ten young professionals stay with the same bank that they opened an account with as student. However, there is no reason why you cannot switch banks – or accounts – to get better service or cheaper banking facilities. Remember that you are the customer, and if you are not satisfied with your banking arrangements you can take your custom elsewhere.

Current Accounts

The Golden Rules

▌ Avoid bank charges whenever possible. Although banks stopped charging those in credit in 1986, some have started to reintroduce fees for packaged accounts that offer a range of services or even for using the branch network. So even if you are in credit you could still pay bank charges.

▌ Be aware that banks and building societies regularly change the terms and conditions of their accounts. These changes may be promoted as a good thing for customers by emphasizing, for instance, that a free overdraft buffer zone of £50 or £100 has been introduced. But read the small print and you may find that charges and overdraft rates have soared.

▌ Earn interest if you keep your account in credit. But never keep large sums in your account as you can get better rates of interest in other types of account.

▌ Never borrow without the consent of your bank because the charges are usually excessive. It will be cheaper to borrow on your credit card than to pay unauthorized overdraft fees.

▌ Always check your bank statements to ensure that they are correct. One recent survey found that one in three customers spot an error every year.

▌ Keep a copy of your bank or building society's latest tariff of charges so that you are fully aware of the financial consequences of being overdrawn or of using any banking facilities.

▌ If you are unhappy with the service or charges of your bank and building society, complain. You may get a refund.

▌ Get to know your bank manager or your personal banker; if your bank is aware of your financial situation it is more likely to be flexible if you suddenly need an additional borrowing facility.

▓ Monitor your bank balance on a regular basis to ensure that you are not overspending or in danger of exceeding your borrowing limits.

▓ If your bank or building society is not helpful – for instance it refuses even a small overdraft – try another bank or building society. Remember that although you do not have an automatic right to an overdraft you are the customer and as a young professional financial institutions should be out to woo your custom.

Choosing the Right Bank Account

You may have a current account that has competitive charges and meets your needs. But the chances are that you would be better off by either switching account or bank.

There is no longer such a thing as a standard current account. With buffer zones (free overdrafts up to a certain limit), interest-bearing current accounts, telephone banking and a myriad of other services it is difficult to compare accounts to find out which one best suits your needs. That is the key: an account that meets your needs, not an account that makes you fit in with the demands of the bank or building society.

Be honest with yourself about what kind of bank customer you are. There is no point opting for an interest-paying current account in the belief that you will be permanently in credit. If you end up being overdrawn for the next six months you could pay more than double the charges of a more suitable bank account.

Evaluating Your Needs

If you are regularly overdrawn:

▪ As a general rule avoid interest-paying current accounts.

▪ If you have high borrowing it may pay to opt for an account with a higher monthly/quarterly fee and lower overdraft interest rates.

▪ If you only borrow small amounts opt for a higher rate of interest and a lower monthly/quarterly fee – the overall cost should be lower.

▪ If you have earnings of around £25,000 a year or more you may be able to opt for a gold card that enables you to borrow up to £10,000 at much lower rates than an overdraft. Although you will have to pay an annual fee this is often comparable with the monthly/quarterly fees charged on current accounts.

If you are occasionally overdrawn:

▪ If your overdraft is small choose an account with a 'buffer zone' – a free overdraft of £50 or £100. However, if you exceed this limit you may find that the borrowing costs – with penalties of up to £50 a month – are far higher than with other current accounts that have a more traditional overdraft facility.

▪ Weigh up the costs of earning interest on your credit balance versus the extra costs of borrowing. Often, interest-paying current accounts have higher overdraft costs than more conventional accounts. So the interest you earn while in credit will only be a fraction of the interest you are paying when overdrawn.

▓ If the borrowing is only small aim to eliminate it altogether by reorganizing your spending habits and monthly budget (see Chapter 1).

▓ If you only dip into the red occasionally you may be better off opting for a daily fee – for instance one of 60p rather than a monthly fee of £8. But if the number of days you are overdrawn exceeds 13 you will generally pay more on the daily fee basis.

▓ Do not forget to agree a borrowing facility with your bank – just because you are only overdrawn occasionally does not mean that you will escape penal bank charges. All overdraft facilities (other than those given automatically with your account) need to be pre-arranged otherwise they are classified as unauthorized borrowing. Some banks do not offer ongoing overdraft facilities but require you to renew overdraft limits.

If you are never overdrawn:

▓ Most banks and building societies offer free banking for those in credit. However, a few do impose some charges, for instance for using other organizations' cash machines, using the branch network or for standing orders and direct debts. You should opt for an account with no charges.

▓ Some banks have introduced accounts with a monthly fee even if you are in credit. In exchange you are offered a range of services. However, you may be better off shopping around for the services and saving the monthly fee.

▓ Opt for an interest-bearing account but never keep substantial amounts of cash in your current account, as you can earn substantially better rates of interest else-where or consider a high-interest cheque account.

Comparing Current Accounts

The first step should be to ask your bank or building society what accounts are on offer. Then pop into another few bank and building society branches to collect copies of their banking tariffs. Then compare the other services that you require. As a busy professional the following are likely to be high priorities:

▪ a range of local cash machines and links to other bank and building society ATMs (Automated Telling Machines)

▪ a branch near your home or place of work

▪ telephone banking facilities so that you can organize your finances in the evening or at weekends when you have more time

▪ cash machines that print mini-statements for better control over your current account

▪ longer opening hours so that you can visit your bank before work, later in the afternoon or on Saturdays

▪ a minimum of a £100 cheque guarantee card - the £50 limit is unlikely to be sufficient to meet your needs

▪ a daily cash withdrawal limit of at least £200

Also take into account personal recommendations. If a colleague or friend has found a particular branch very helpful you should take this advice into account.

To compare the financial costs of a current account do the following:

1   Look through your past three to six months bank statements to calculate your average overdraft. Interest is charged on a daily basis. However, calculating an exact figure takes a long time and an average will give you a good ballpark figure to work with.

2   Compare the interest rates and bank charges on the current accounts you are considering. Interest rates at the time of publishing varied from under 9 per cent to over 23 per cent. Some accounts charge per transaction. But most have a set fee that can range from £2 to £10 per month or £3 to £15 per quarter.

    Remember, charges can be far more expensive than the interest. For instance you may be charged a monthly £8 fee for borrowing £200 for three days. The interest charged will be a fraction of this so you may be better off opting for an account with either a lower or no monthly fee and a higher overdraft interest rate.

    Often, there are arrangement fees for overdrafts of 1 or 2 per cent, with a minimum charge of up to £15.

3   Compare when charges are levied. If you dip into the red once a quarter and are charged on a quarterly basis you will have to pay the maximum bank charges for the entire year. But if you opt for an account with monthly charges you will only have to pay the fee four times a year.

    Also, check when charging periods start and finish. You could find that this is just before you are paid, so you will be overdrawn at the end of one charging period and the beginning of the next, and as such will pay two lots of overdraft fees instead of one.

4   Calculate how much different accounts will cost you.
    For example, Mr Spender usually dips £350 into the red at the end of each month for an average of ten days.
    Bank account A charges him interest of 21 per cent per annum plus a monthly fee of £8. It also charges him a fee to arrange his overdraft. Over a year his bank charges add up as follows:

> Total interest: £24
> + the monthly fee of £8 × 12 months = £96
> + £15 overdraft arrangement fee
> = Total cost: £135

Bank account B has no charges other than interest at 21 per cent.

> Total cost: £24

The Consumers' Association recently calculated that a borrower with a £500 unauthorized overdraft for one week each quarter would pay £300 per year with one bank but just £65 with another.
    Even on authorized (agreed) overdrafts the difference is vast. The annual cost of going overdrawn by £500 for one week each quarter varies from £3.50 with one building society to £150.35 with one bank.

£ CASH TIP £

Unauthorized overdrafts over a short period of time can have an equivalent annual percentage rate of more than 2000 per cent. So borrowing on a credit card will be far, far cheaper.

£ CASH TIP £

It is easy to dip into the red unintentionally because your money is stuck in the clearing system. Be aware of the time it takes to clear cheques (usually three working days) and cash (it will not usually be credited to your account until the next working day). Building societies have even longer clearing delays. Remember that if you pay by debit card the amount may be taken out of your account after one day instead of the three-day period for clearing cheques.

£ CASH TIP £

You should be aware of the charges that your bank will make for unauthorized overdrafts just in case you exceed your overdraft limit by accident. Some banks charge £25 each time you use your cheque guarantee card or debit card, and others charge a set fee of say £3.50 for each day you exceed your limits on top of the flat monthly fee.

Switching Current Accounts

Ignore the negative propaganda about the difficulties involved in switching bank accounts. It should be straight-forward provided you follow the correct procedure.

1   Choose the account and bank or building society branch that best suits your needs.

2   Open a new account before closing the old one. Even if you are angry with your bank do not close your existing account until you are ready. The switch usually takes four to six weeks.

To open a bank or building society account you will need to provide identification (your passport, driving licence or national insurance card), proof of your address (often bills or bank statements), and often your pay slips or a letter of reference from your employers.

3   Once your account has been processed (usually at least four days) and you have sufficient funds in your new account you should be given a cash card automatically. You may have to wait a little longer to receive a cheque guarantee card or debit card, and if you require an overdraft you will usually be required to have your salary paid directly into your new account.

4   Select a date for your account to be switched. Allow plenty of time to ensure that you have informed all the relevant organizations. Write to your employer saying that you are switching accounts and give details so that your salary can be paid into the new account from the switch date (ideally you should switch on the date when you are next paid).

5   Obtain a list of standing orders and direct debits from your existing bank (check that there is no fee) or look through past bank or building society statements.

6   Write to your existing bank or building society and ask them to cancel all standing orders from the transfer date. Send a list of your standing orders to your new bank asking them to pay them from the new date; also, write to the payees to tell them you are switching accounts, giving details.

7   Write to all the organizations to whom you pay direct debits asking for a new mandate form. You will need to complete a separate form for each direct debit. Send

the forms to your new bank and ask them to pay the direct debits from the transfer date. Contact your old bank and instruct them not to pay any more direct debits as from the transfer date.

8   Keep some funds in your old bank account after the switching date just in case any cheques have not cleared.

9   Once you have received your new cheque book, cheque and ATM card, and are happy with your new account, you can then close the old account and either ask for the outstanding balance to be transferred to your new account or, if you are in the red, pay off your overdraft with the new one. You will need to return unused cheques and plastic cards.

How to Complain

Complain to your bank as soon as you spot the error and ask for any wrongly charged interest or fees to be refunded or lost interest to be repaid. Often, the branch manager has the discretion to make small payments to cover losses and inconvenience caused by a banking error. Ask for a copy of the Banking Code from your bank to find out how its complaints procedure works.

As with all complaints, keep a copy of your correspondence. If you still do not receive satisfaction after making your complaint, write to the customer relations or complaints department at your bank or building society's head office. Only after you have exhausted the bank's complaints procedure can you contact the Banking or Building Society Ombudsman to take up your case (see Chapter 11).

3 Borrowing

There is a fine line between credit and debt.

As a young professional the chances are that an overdraft and credit card will be vital to financing your lifestyle even if only for short periods of time.

Before you borrow money always think about how much you can afford to repay each month – not just how much a lender will offer to lend you – and if you could still meet these payments if interest rates were to rise. If you cannot meet your repayments your borrowing costs will rise as you may have to pay interest on your outstanding interest, may be charged financial penalties and in the worst scenario you could be taken to court or have your home repossessed.

Many of those who borrow on their credit card or run up an overdraft also have savings and investments. However, it does not make financial sense as you would need to earn a fantastic rate of return on your investments to cover the cost of interest and charges. Borrowing £1000 on a credit card costs around £200 a year. You would need to earn 20 per cent returns after tax or 34 per before tax as a higher rate taxpayer on £1000 of savings just to break even.

Comparing the Cost of Borrowing

The Annual Percentage Rate (APR) is the true cost of interest over a year and includes interest and one-off charges.

However, it does not include credit insurance, which many lenders push customers into buying. The lower the APR the better the deal.

Choosing the Best Way of Borrowing

How Long Do You Want to Borrow For?

Short-term: Overdrafts or credit cards may work out cheaper than personal loans. Overdrafts linked to gold charge cards can also be good value but do not forget to take into account the annual fee.

Longer term (a year or more): Personal loans and secured loans.

Do You Want to Make a Set Repayment Every Month?

If you are unsure as to whether or not you will be able to make a fixed repayment each month you may be better off opting for a more flexible type of borrowing such as a credit card or overdraft.

If you intend to repay your borrowing quickly you should watch for financial penalties with personal loans, as in some cases you may have to pay some of the interest you would have paid had you not repaid your loan early. This means you are paying interest on money you no longer owe.

The Borrowing Options

Overdrafts

You may be surprised the find out that an overdraft can be one of the cheapest forms of borrowing over the shorter term.

Provided you agree the overdraft in advance and have a bank account with no – or a low – monthly or quarterly overdraft fee and a low rate of interest you may find that an overdraft is cheaper than a loan.

Credit Cards

Credit cards are ideal for short-term borrowing and the high level of competition between card issuers means that you can pay far less interest on your credit card than on your overdraft. If you borrow £2000 on a credit card for a year, it can cost as little as £100 or more than £360, so shop around.

Beware of borrowing long-term using a credit card as the costs can mount up and you may be better off opting for a personal loan or increasing your mortgage.

Comparing the costs of borrowing

With most types of borrowing you can simply compare the annual percentage rate (APR). However with credit cards this is not so reliable because interest is charged from different dates – some card issuers charge from the date of purchase, some from the day it is noted on your account, and some from the date of your statement. Yet credit cards with the same interest rate and annual fee will have the same APR no matter how interest is charged. APRs at the time of going to press varied from 11 to 30 per cent and annual fees from nil to £20. So you should also look at the monthly interest rate, compare annual fees, and take into account when and how interest is charged.

You will also need to evaluate special offers. To attract new customers some credit card issuers now often waive the annual fee in the first year or offer to wipe off a percentage of your existing credit card balance.

If you pay off your credit card bill in full each month you will be better off opting for a card with no annual fee and a higher rate of interest. As you will not be paying interest your credit card will be free.

If you borrow only a small amount on your credit card for short periods you may be better off opting for a card with no or a low annual fee and a higher rate of interest.

If you borrow large sums on your credit card for long periods you will be better off paying an annual fee and opting for a much lower rate of interest.

How to avoid paying interest

Most credit cards have interest-free periods, which means that if you settle the outstanding balance *in full* within this period – usually up to 56 days – you pay no interest at all.

Be aware of the time it takes for your payment to reach your credit card account – often seven working days if you are paying by post. If you miss this payment date by just one day you will forfeit your interest free period and pay interest on the total outstanding amount. Interest is charged on a daily basis so even if you miss the payment deadline you can still cut your costs of borrowing by clearing or reducing your outstanding borrowing as soon as you can.

The best days to pay by credit card are on or just after the statement date (printed at the top of your monthly statement). If you spend on that date the item will not appear on your credit card statement for a further month, so you will have 15 to 25 days from then in which to settle your bill without paying interest. If you use your credit card just before your statement date your interest-free period will be reduced by up to a month. The rules vary from credit card to credit card so make sure you are fully aware of the terms and conditions.

£ CASH TIP £

Do not use your credit card to draw cash from a bank or cash machine unless you have to, as you will usually be charged 1 or 2 per cent of the amount of cash withdrawn with a minimum fee of around £1.50. And you will forfeit the interest-free period as interest is usually charged from the date you withdraw the cash.

The benefits of a credit card

If you buy faulty goods costing more than £100 using your credit card you should be protected under the Consumer Credit Act, which makes the card issuer jointly liable with the retailer. In effect, if you buy a faulty item of equipment and the retailer refuses to give you a refund you can ask your card issuer to give you the refund instead. So if a travel company or shop goes bust before you have taken the holiday or received the goods, you will not lose out.

Some credit card issuers offer free purchase protection – an insurance against theft or accidental damage (often for up to ninety days after purchase) – covering the goods you have bought with your credit card. Also, credit cards have the added protection that if they are lost or stolen you are usually only liable for the first £50 of losses (unlike cash). But remember, you are required to report loss or theft immediately. Read the terms of your credit card to ensure that you are aware of your responsibilities.

£ CASH TIP £

Always check your credit card statement – errors are rare but they can be made.

£ CASH TIP £

Always check that your credit card slip has been filled in correctly. Although most credit card transactions are now electronic, if a payment slip is used £100 can easily be written as £1000 by mistake or if you fail to fill in the final figure it is easy for someone to add a few extra pounds to your bill. And ask for the carbon copies of the card payment slip (particularly when travelling abroad) as it has been known for fraudsters to use this information to duplicate a card.

Managing your credit

Remember that if you do not pay your balance in full each month you will still have to repay a minimum of 3 to 5 per cent of your balance each month.

£ CASH TIP £

Some card issuers now fine cardholders who exceed their card limits (£15 in some cases) or fail to make the minimum repayments (for example £20 for two months overdue and a further £20 for people three months overdue). Once these charges are added, borrowing costs can spiral.

Switching credit cards

If you transfer your outstanding balance to another credit card you can often get a better deal. This can include 5 per cent being wiped off your outstanding balance or no fee and a reduced rate of interest for one year. However, after these benefits have been taken you may find you are then paying over-the-odds for your credit card. If the new card issuer will not give you the same borrowing limit, it may not pay you to switch to a new card.

£ CASH TIP £

If you threaten to switch to a different card issuer and say that this is because of the introduction or size of the annual fee, you may find that your existing credit card issuer will agree to waive the fee for one year.

Credit cards with cheque books

An increasing number of credit card issuers are offering cheque books linked to credit cards. This enables cardholders to make purchases where credit cards are not accepted or where retailers charge an extra fee for paying with a credit card. The cheque book can also be used to pay off money owed to other card issuers or to clear an overdraft or loan. However, spending by cheque could cost you a 1.5 per cent charge. This extra charge, or a fee of say 75p, often makes credit card cheques a more expensive way to pay, and there is often no interest-free period for cheque transactions. Although a preferential interest rate is often offered, this can outweigh the other extra costs.

Becoming a caring cardholder

Affinity/charity cards are credit cards linked to charities or other organizations that enable you to donate money to charity or another worthy cause every time you make a purchase with your credit card. Typically, 25p in every £100 you spend goes to the good cause and some card issuers also give an initial donation of £5.

Charge Cards

Credit cards require that you pay a minimum amount (usually 5 per cent of the outstanding balance) to service your credit each month. Charge cards require you to pay the *full* balance every month by direct debit so no interest is charged. Instead you pay an annual subscription fee. If you fail to settle your bill there will normally be a financial penalty and you also run the risk that your card will be withdrawn if this happens too often.

Although you cannot get extended credit on a charge card, many cards offer a preferential interest rate on an overdraft. At the time of going to press it was possible to borrow up to £10,000 at 10 per cent. So for large borrowers the lower interest costs compensate for the high annual fee that can be around £80. This fee often includes a range of other services such as purchase protection or Air Miles.

Charge cards do not have the same low pre-set spending limits as credit cards and so you do not have to worry about running over your limit.

Gold Cards

These can either be credit or charge cards and have the added advantage of extra services and, in the case of credit cards, a higher credit limit. However, annual fees can be much higher.

To qualify for a gold card you will need to have annual earnings of at least £20,000 a year.

If you do not borrow on a gold card, it is an expensive addition to your wallet. Although you may benefit from extra services and a higher spending limit, at the end of the day what you are really paying for is the privilege of flashing a gold card.

Additional services can include travel or accident insurance, emergency cash and card replacements, legal and medical helplines, compensation for luggage delays or losses, and a refund of money spent on holiday when a travel company fails. Some cards also offer extended warranties on electrical items purchased with the card, Air Miles, discounts, and a range of other perks.

Store Cards

If you tend to use your credit card at only two or three shops and pay off your outstanding balance in full each month, a store card could be more cost effective than a credit card. Although the rate of interest charged on store cards is usually higher than that charged on credit cards, if you never borrow money on your card the rate will be irrelevant. And store cards do not have an annual fee.

The advantages are that you can usually get discounts or special shopping benefits as a store card holder, and in some cases store cards may be the only type of credit card accepted in a shop.

Personal Loans

If you intend to borrow over the longer term, in most cases you will be better off with a personal loan than an overdraft or credit card. However, it is essential that you shop around for the best rate as in some cases overdraft interest rates are the same as personal loan rates.

Personal loans are usually spread over one, two or five years, with the interest rate fixed over the set term.

Some companies now offer more flexible loans that allow you to repay what you want each month, provided that you repay the loan within a set period of time and repay a minimum percentage (often 2 to 4 per cent) each month.

All APRs must be worked out in the same way, including interest and other charges, and taking into account how and when payments are made. However, extras such as credit protection insurance may not be included. Watch out for arrangement fees, as they can push up the costs of borrowing.

£ CASH TIP £

Ask if there are any penalties if you pay off your loan early. For instance you may be charged interest for an extra two months rather than for just the time period for which you have borrowed the money. So be careful not to take out a loan for longer than you need.

£ CASH TIP £

You may not be given a written quotation detailing the costs and terms of the loan but you must be given one if you ask. It is better to read it at home when you have time to study it carefully. Most loan application forms include some form of credit protection insurance but you may have to tick a box if you _do not_ want it rather than opting for it.

£ CASH TIP £

You cannot cancel a credit deal if you sign it in a trader's shop, office, or other business premises. You can only cancel if you signed the form at home. Unless you can see a box entitled 'Your right to cancel' you will not be able to do so. Be wary of agreeing deals over the phone. You may not be able to cancel a credit agreement arranged on the phone, even if you sign it at home.

Credit with Purchases

Often you will find that shops, double glazing companies, kitchen manufacturers and car showrooms offer credit facilities. Unless the credit is interest-free or at a preferentially low rate, you should be aware that the interest rates may be higher than those of a bank loan.

If you pay off your loan early, you may find that you have to pay some of the interest you would have had to pay should the loan have run its full term. However, this is often confusingly called a 'rebate' of the interest you would have paid. A rebate may sound like you are benefiting but you are not – the extra interest you must pay is in effect a penalty.

Always read the small print and read through the terms and conditions before signing.

Interest-free Credit

Be aware that the cost of free credit may be built into the price of the goods you are purchasing. You could find that you may be better off buying cheaper goods without interest-free credit as the savings may be greater than the costs of taking out a loan, overdraft or paying by credit card.

Often a deposit of 10 to 25 per cent must be paid. Check what will happen if you cannot make the payments. If you do not repay the loan within the interest-free period you may then pay a very high rate of interest.

Buy Now, Pay Later

Increasingly, retailers are offering deals with 'nothing to pay for a year'. However, in some cases a deposit is required. Check what rates of interest are charged once the nothing-to-pay period has ended, as often the rates are very high. If you still want to take up one of these offers borrow the money for free and when the free period ends settle the loan in full by taking out a loan from a cheaper lender.

Secured Loans

These are normally cheaper than unsecured ones. Remember although 'secured' sounds like a safe way to borrow, it is only safe for the lender because the loan is secured on an asset – usually your home – and if you fail to keep up repayments you are at risk of losing your home.

Rates tend to be lower than for other types of loan and repayments are lower because the loan is usually over a longer period. Weigh up the pitfalls of securing the loan on your home against the savings in borrowing costs, and do not forget to take into account any extra costs such as valuation and legal fees.

You can either approach your mortgage lender for a further advance on your mortgage – which will probably be the cheapest option – or approach a separate lender.

In some cases you can use other assets such as endowment policies as security for a loan (ask your life insurance company for details).

Staff Loans

Many large employers offer interest-free loans for the purchase of season tickets. These are tax free and the only limitation is that you have to use them for to pay for a season ticket to travel to work. If you have other borrowings, consider taking out a staff loan and reducing your other debts.

Hire Purchase

Hire purchase (HP) is credit offered so that you can make an instant purchase (although you do not initially own the goods) and is often offered on electrical goods and cars. The monthly interest rates and APR can be very high and a bank loan will probably be cheaper. To pull out of an HP agreement after the cancellation period (the first few days or weeks in which you can cancel the agreement) you must pay or have paid at least half of the total costs, be up-to-date with your payments and you must return the goods. If they are damaged you will probably have to pay for repairs. You cannot sell HP goods until the agreement has been paid off.

A new form of hire purchase 'Option to own', allows you to pay for the goods over two to four years, and either own them after that period or, within the payment period, take an option to upgrade to a newer model. APRs can be as high as 30 per cent and often you are also required to pay for insurance to cover the cost of repairs.

Credit/Payment Protection Plans

If you are borrowing a significant amount of money you will probably be recommended to take out payment protection insurance by the person or company arranging your loan. This covers your payments should you lose your job because of illness or if you are made redundant.

However, in some cases you may not even qualify for your loans to be repaid so, as always, you should read the small print very carefully. In some cases you may not be given full policy details or you may be pressured into taking out this insurance as a 'condition' of the loan. However, as sales representatives often receive a commission for selling these insurance policies check first whether it is essential that you take out a policy.

In most cases you cannot claim against the policy in the first few weeks or months, and when you do claim you may have to wait a certain period (ie you must be unemployed for more than so many weeks or months) before your loan is repaid or monthly repayments are made on your behalf. There may be a condition that you have to be in employment for a certain minimum period to qualify, so if you move jobs you may invalidate your policy. If you are a part-time worker or self-employed you may also be excluded.

You can shop around to find a policy that will cover your needs or one that is cheaper. However, sometimes the best credit and loan rates depend on your buying this insurance.

In some cases you may not be able to cancel the insurance policy should you repay your loan early, so you may be required to pay the premiums even though you no longer have a loan.

In general, payment protection costs around 70p for each £100 of borrowing on credit cards and up to a fifth of the repayments on a personal loan.

Your Credit Rating

When you apply for credit, you will be assessed to decide whether you are a suitable risk.

Credit Scoring

It can be very embarrassing to walk into a shop, be offered instant credit and then suffer the humiliation of having your credit application refused. However, this does not necessarily mean that you have a poor credit history. Up to half of all loan applications are refused.

Credit scoring is the system that ensures that the borrower meets certain lending criteria. Lenders have a profile of the type of customer that they have calculated is a good risk. Generally, if you have only been in your current job for a few months, are not on the electoral roll, do not have a telephone, have not lived at the same address for a certain length of time and have no other credit, you may find it harder to borrow.

Information normally comes from a questionnaire you have to fill in that will ask questions such as 'Are you a homeowner?' and 'How long have you been in your current employment?'. In addition, information from credit reference agencies is taken into account. These agencies keep files on almost every adult in the UK and information includes any county court judgements for non-payment and details of how you have managed your other borrowing.

Up to thirty factors are used in credit scoring, so being turned down by one lender does not necessarily mean that you will be refused by another.

The lender does not have to tell you exactly why it has refused you credit but should give you an indication of the reason. If you think that a lender's decision to refuse you credit is unjustified or wrong, and that there is further relevant information that may change the lender's mind, you should ask the lender how to go about having the decision reviewed.

Checking Your Credit Reference

If you are refused credit for £15,000 or less you have a legal right to know the name and address of any credit reference agency that was approached for details about you. To find out which credit reference agency was used you need to write to the shop or loan company that refused you credit and ask for the name of the reference agency. You must write within 28 days of the last time you contacted the retailer (or other organization) about the credit deal and they must tell you the name and address of the reference agency within seven working days. If an agency was not used, you do not have to be sent a reply.

When you contact the credit reference agency you must send £1 and give your full name and address with postcode and any addresses you have lived at during the past six years. It then has seven working days to send you your file or tell you it has no information about you.

If you feel that the facts on your file are incorrect write to the agency asking them to remove or amend the entry that you think is wrong. Within 28 days the agency should confirm that it will remove or alter the entry or state why it will take no action. If the agency has replied in that time you can send a 'notice of correction' to add to your credit reference file.

Often the problem is that you are affected by others who live in your household such as your spouse, flatmate or even past residents if they have a poor credit history. Relatives with the same surname and address can ask for their records to be 'dissociated'.

If the agency amends your file or adds a notice of correction it must send the details to anybody who has enquired about your credit rating during the previous six months.

The two main credit reference agencies are:

CCN Group Ltd
Consumer Help Service
PO Box 40
Nottingham
NG7 2SS

Equifax Europe UK Ltd
Dept 1E
PO Box 3001
Glasgow
G81 2DT

Contacts

If you have a problem with a credit reference agency contact the Office of Fair Trading on 0171 211 8000. The OFT also produces useful booklets on credit and debt. Call 0181 957 5058 for further information. For free help if you have problems paying for credit, contact your local Citizens Advice Bureau.

4 *Saving*

Keep something for a rainy day.

At a time in your life when your finances are likely to be stretched saving may be a low priority. But you should aim to have at least three month's salary saved to cover emergencies from redundancy to a major household repair.

If you have borrowings you must bear in mind that you will be paying interest of up to twenty times more on these debts than you will earn on your savings. However, this does not take into account human nature. If you are the sort of person who lives on the edge, spending up to the limit on your overdraft and credit card, a savings account could bail you out if you get into financial trouble.

As with all other financial products you must keep a regular watch on the rates of return. Even if you shop around to get the best savings rate today, the chances are that in a few months time you could get a far better deal elsewhere.

New and tough competition in the savings market from telephone and postal savings organizations to supermarkets means that by shopping around you can easily earn three times as much interest as in a standard savings account.

There are several ways to achieve a higher savings rate, but most accounts that offer higher rates of return also require you to tie up your cash for long periods or impose penalties for early withdrawal of your savings. Generally, the more you invest the higher the rate.

Bank and Building Society Saving Accounts

These are the main types of account on offer. Some accounts may be a mixture of one or more of the following:

Deposit Accounts

Run by banks these generally offer poor rates for smaller sums. The advantage is that you can easily switch money from a deposit account into your current account, or vice versa.

Instant Access Accounts

These are ideal if you may need to get your hands on your savings in a hurry. It is essential to shop around as rates vary widely, £1000 invested in an instant access account over the last five years would have earned you around £190 in interest in a poor earning account and almost £400 in a top paying account.

High-interest Cheque Accounts

These offer better rates than those of ordinary interest-bearing current accounts but the rates are not always that much higher and those with low balances can still earn less than 1 per cent interest and in some cases no interest at all on small balances of below £2000. The advantage is that you get a cheque book.

Notice Accounts

These generally require that you give thirty, sixty or ninety days notice before you withdraw your savings in return for a higher rate of interest. If you need your money sooner you will lose interest already earned over a period equivalent to the notice period. Some accounts offer one withdrawal free of penalty every six months or every quarter. Again, it pays to shop around. A recent survey by *Which? Magazine* found that £10,000 invested over five years in the top paying account would have earned £4584 in interest, but £1000 less in a poorer paying account with a big high-street bank.

Postal/Telephone Accounts

These offer higher rates of return because, in theory, the building societies and other deposit-takers that operate these accounts do not have to charge you a proportion of the expenses of running a branch network. Rates are also higher because these accounts are often only open to investors for a short period of time. Again, these accounts have tiered rates of interest and there are higher rates for those prepared to give a longer notice period. Some require minimum deposits of £1000 or more.

Tiered Rate Accounts

Most accounts pay more to those with larger sums. Always be aware of the point at which interest rates rise; it can mean an instant access account pays more for a £5000 deposit than a notice account pays on the same sum. If you withdraw savings make sure you do not drop down to the next tier of interest and be aware that some accounts pay no or very low interest on smaller sums.

Regular Savings Accounts

These pay a higher rate of interest if you are prepared to invest a regular amount every month. Some allow only one or two withdrawals a year and others pay a bonus if there are no withdrawals in a year. Often a set amount must be invested for a set term (for instance three years) in order to qualify for a higher rate of interest. But any withdrawals could result in interest penalties.

Term Accounts

If you are prepared to commit your money for six months to five years you can get a higher rate of interest in a term account. Many offer fixed rates, so if rates are likely to rise (as they did in the spring and summer of 1997) you may find that a fixed account over a longer period is not a good investment. There are large penalties for early withdrawal. Minimum investments are usually £2000. These accounts are also known as bonds.

Escalator Bonds

These pay a predetermined rising rate of interest over an agreed term – usually five years. At the time of going to press minimum investments ranged from £500 to £5000 and rates started at around 6 per cent gross in year one rising to 10 per cent by the fifth year, giving an average rate of interest of 7.75 per cent gross. Check for penalties for early withdrawals. In some cases withdrawals are not allowed. In return you will receive a higher rate of interest. Most operate over a five-year term although some are three-year bonds.

Offshore Accounts

Offshore branches of the larger banks and building societies pay interest without tax deducted. But that does not mean that you can avoid paying tax – it must be declared on your tax return. Most branches are based in the Channel Islands or the Isle of Man. The advantage is that you earn interest on the amount of tax due until you have to pay your tax bill, giving you use of this for up to twenty months. Rates are usually slightly higher than equivalent accounts offered in the UK.

Accounts That Pay Bonuses

A variety of accounts including the tax-exempt savings account (TESSA), offer bonuses to lock in your cash and encourage loyalty. Rates are likely to be higher than average, but if you withdraw your money before the bonus is paid, your rate of return will be far lower.

Compound Interest Accounts

You can boost the returns on a savings account by earning interest on interest already credited to your account – known as compounding. The frequency of interest payments is therefore important. One account may pay 5 per cent annually but another 5 per cent monthly, giving a compound annual rate (CAR) of 5.12 per cent.

Money Market Bank Accounts

The money markets are where large financial institutions put their billions of pounds on deposit overnight to make extra profits and are not usually open to smaller investors. But by pooling cash from a large number of customers, financial institutions can offer access to the same attractive rates. These are a mixture of savings accounts and cheque accounts. The minimum investment is usually £5000.

TESSAs

Tax-Exempt Special Savings Accounts are tax free provided you invest for five years. But they will no longer be available from April 1999 when a new tax-efficient savings scheme, the Individual Savings Account, is introduced. Those with existing TESSA accounts will be able to switch to the new scheme.

You can only have one TESSA account and you have to be over 18 to open one. The maximum investments are: £3000 in the first year and up to £1800 in the subsequent years up to an overall maximum of £9000. Minimum investments are as low as £10. But to get the best rates you normally have to invest the maximum.

Over the last five years you could have earned £700 more in interest by picking a top paying TESSA compared to the poorest payer from one of the big four high-street banks. You can either have a fixed or variable rate (fixed rates are not a good idea if interest rates are set to rise).

Feeder accounts

Although you can only invest £3000 in the first year, some accounts allow you to invest the full £9000 and pay a higher rate as a result. £6000 is invested in a feeder account earning taxable interest and £3000 in the TESSA. Then on every anniversary the permitted maximum is transferred from the feeder account into the TESSA.

Bonuses

Comparing TESSA accounts can be difficult because many rely on bonuses to boost returns. These are usually added at the end of the five-year investment term and are designed to discourage savers from switching to another, higher-paying TESSA account.

Equity linked

These are a newer type of TESSA and offer a low guaranteed return but the potential of higher yields if the stock market performs well.

What if I need my money?

You can withdraw some of the interest you have earned but must leave enough interest in the TESSA to cover the 20 per cent tax that should be deducted. If you withdraw any capital you will lose all the tax benefits and your TESSA will be closed. You may also have to pay an early encashment penalty.

Choosing a Savings Account

The golden rule is to shop around. Check your rates regularly to ensure you are still earning the highest rates. *The Daily Telegraph* and other newspapers and magazines print lists of the best savings rates. You can also check rates on Teletext or Ceefax.

Warning: Savers are losing million of pounds in interest by keeping their money in accounts that no longer pay a competitive rate of interest and are obsolete because they are no longer open to new savers. Your building society or bank may advertise attractive rates but these often only apply to new savers. However, the new Banking Code requires banks and building societies to write to those with obsolete accounts at least once a year giving a list of the alternative savings rates. The Banking Code is available from your local bank or building society.

£ CASH TIPS £

£ Consolidate accounts – you will be better off pooling money as generally the more you invest, the higher the rate.

£ If you are planning to switch account always give the notice required or you will lose interest. Check if there are any transfer penalties or if you will lose any bonuses, as these financial penalties could wipe out any extra interest you will earn from a higher paying account.

£ Always shop around for the best rates. Often smaller building societies perform better than the larger ones and the big high-street banks.

£ Always check the competitiveness of your savings account on a regular basis. There are millions of pounds tied up in dormant accounts that no longer pay a competitive rate of interest.

£ Remember that once tax has been deducted from your interest it can be hard to beat inflation particularly if you are a higher rate taxpayer. This means that over the long-run your savings will go down in value in 'real terms'.

Building Society Conversions

Carpetbaggers is the name given to those investing in a building society in the hope that it will convert from being a mutual to a bank and offer free shares (as the Woolwich and Halifax have done). Some deposit accounts do not confer voting rights and as such do not qualify for windfall payouts. If you are planning to gamble on a building society conversion, check that the account will qualify for shares. Be prepared to invest a much larger deposit, often £2000 or more, as those tipped to offer free shares have been flooded by saver's cash and are trying to discourage smaller savers from opening accounts.

Tax and Savings

If you do not pick a tax-free savings scheme, tax will generally be deducted from any interest you earn before it is credited to your savings account (the exceptions to this are offshore accounts, TESSAs and some National Savings accounts).

Tax is deducted at 20 per cent – the lower rate of tax. Only higher rate or 40 per cent taxpayers have to pay any additional tax. So that means that 23 per cent taxpayers only have to pay 20 per cent tax on their savings. If for some reason you become a non-taxpayer you can reclaim the 20 per cent tax deducted from your interest.

National Savings

These are often overlooked. However, as some of the savings schemes are tax free they should at least be considered for part of your cash. Most of the products – particularly the longer-term fixed-rate schemes – will probably not appeal to the young professional.

Tax free schemes include:

Index-linked savings certificates: These pay a fixed amount of interest (2.75 per cent at the time of publishing) above the rate of inflation, have £100 minimum investment, and are tax free, but must be held for five years.

Savings certificates: These pay a guaranteed rate of return (5.35 per cent compound at the time of publishing), must be held for five years, and are also tax free.

Ordinary accounts: The first £70 of interest is tax free but the rates are often low (starting at 1.5 per cent at the time of publishing).

Premium bonds: There is no guarantee that you will earn anything. However, the prize money paid out is equivalent to 4.75 per cent interest a year. The minimum investment is just £100 and all prizes are tax free. The odds are better than the lottery at 19,000 to 1.

The National Savings Sales Information Unit is on 0645 645000.

5 *Investment Advice*

Seek wise counsel.

Investing, rather than saving, is the only way to build up a sizeable lump sum and beat inflation over the medium to long-term. But it is also one of the most difficult aspects of personal finance to understand and one of the hardest to get right.

There is a bewildering choice of products on offer, performance and charges vary from company to company, and if you make the wrong decision you could lose thousands of pounds – either because the value of your investment falls or because you could have made much larger gains if you had picked a better performing investment.

Although it is possible to be your own financial adviser it takes time and effort. Newspapers and magazines produce performance charts so you can compare how good companies are at investing their clients' money. But you will also need to know how good a company's administration is, how its charges compare, and how financially sound it is.

That is why you should seek professional advice. Remember, you can ask more than one adviser for an opinion but at the end of the day any investment decision is ultimately yours.

The difficulty is finding a financial adviser you can trust and who meets your needs. There is no shortage of advice available – some 75,000 individuals are authorized to give investment advice.

But before you select a financial adviser you must know how the financial services industry is regulated. These investor protection rules are designed to protect your interests and, if the worst happens, to compensate you for any losses if a firm goes bust while owing you money.

Investor Protection

The financial services industry is self regulating. The chief city watchdog is the Securities and Investments Board, which oversees the Self-Regulatory Organizations (SROs). The main regulator for companies selling investments to individuals is the Personal Investment Authority (PIA). You may also deal with a firm that is a member of the Investment Management Regulatory Organization (IMRO), which oversees fund managers, or the Securities and Futures Authority (SFA), which regulates stockbrokers and futures and options dealers.

Members of recognized professional bodies can also give investment advice. These include: solicitors who are regulated by the Law Society; accountants who are members of the various accounting bodies, including the Institute of Chartered Accountants and the Chartered Association of Certified Accounts; and insurance brokers who are members of the Insurance Brokers Registration Council.

Currently there are ten different bodies regulating the financial services sector. However, this is set to change with the SIB taking over regulation of the banks and merging with its main subsidiary regulatory agencies to form the Investor Protection Agency some time in late 1998 or early 1999. The new super-regulator may not take responsibility for building societies or insurance companies. However, all investment business by banks, building societies and insurance companies is already covered by the SIB.

SIMON J LANDER & CO LTD is an independent Financial Adviser and a member of Countrywide Independent Advisers Ltd which is regulated by the Personal Investment Authority for Life Assurance, Pensions and Investment Business only. Simon J Lander & Co Ltd has been a member of Countrywide since December 1994 and is provided with in-depth product research and compliance assistance together with a number of 'branded' products and enhanced product terms.

Simon Lander, our Managing Director, founded Simon J Lander & Co Ltd in 1987 and is committed to providing each and every client with not only a professional service, but also one that is tailored to suit each client's individual requirements. Simon J Lander & Co Ltd specialises in offering full financial planning solutions which can be altered at the various life stages to suit client needs.

Typically advice will cover a broad range of topics from pension planning, family protection, wealth creation, income protection, tax mitigation and mortgage arrangements. Not only is this advice relevant to individuals, but also partnerships, directors and limited companies, all of which will have important financial issues which will require advice throughout their lives. It is our experience that successful individuals and corporate organisations are often unable to allocate sufficient time to consider their financial well-being, as the emotive subject of financial services can be put off until tomorrow. In reality, however, tomorrow never comes and spending some time discussing and taking appropriate action for protection and investing in the future can help remove some financial constraints and worries, immediately the appropriate arrangements are made. Not all areas of advice we give or contracts we recommend are regulated by the Personal Investment Authority.

As one may now expect, technology plays a large part in the company and using software programmes to take care of some basic functions assists greatly in the smooth running of client management. However, initial fact finding skills based on traditional question, answer and discussion techniques are still considered to be the most appropriate method of establishing a rapport and gathering the required knowledge to proceed and provide appropriate financial advice.

Simon J Lander & Co Ltd specialise in building long term relationships with its clients and although most of its clientele are situated in the London, South East and East Anglian regions, it has clients scattered all over the world.

Independent Financial Advisers specialising in London, East Anglia and the South East for professional individual service on

- *PENSIONS*
- *LIFE ASSURANCE*
- *SAVINGS AND INVESTMENTS*
- *ILLNESS PROTECTION**
- *MORTGAGE ARRANGEMENTS**

To discuss your requirements call
Simon Lander or Mike Passfield at

SIMON J LANDER & CO LTD
22 High Street
Saffron Walden
Essex
CB10 1AX

Tel: 0800 378411
Fax: 01799 513919

A member of Countrywide Independent Advisers Ltd which is regulated by the Personal Investment Authority for Life Assurance, Pensions and Investment Business only.

*The PIA does not regulate these services

The regulators not only check that companies are financially sound but also monitor training (all advisers must now pass exams), advertising, marketing, and the quality of investment advice.

The Investors' Compensation Scheme is the final protection but it only pays out if a firm goes bust owing clients money. The maximum compensation is £48,000 (so larger investors may lose out) and it does not compensate for poor investment returns or poor advice.

The Financial Services Act has limitations and does not cover all financial products, only:

▪ personal pensions

▪ endowment policies

▪ life insurance investments such as equity bonds

▪ PEPs, unit trusts and investment trusts

▪ shares and share-based investments

Products *not* covered include:

▪ mortgages

▪ savings

▪ company pension schemes

▪ general insurance (such as household and motor)

Different Types of Financial Adviser

Advisers are polarized into two types, although some companies have different branches and as such can offer both types of advice.

Independent Financial Advisers

These, as the name implies, are independent of any one investment company or other financial organisation although they may be employed by one (some banks and building societies have independent financial advice services). Some 21,000 individuals in the UK are authorized to give independent advice. This means they must compare a range of financial products from a range of companies before recommending an investment. However, they do earn commission from any company whose products they sell.

Fee-earning financial advisers charge you a fee for advice and rebate any commission they would earn (usually by adding this commission to your investment). Accountants and solicitors work on a fee basis. You should find that paying a fee is financially worthwhile. The only drawback is that if you decide not to invest you will still have to pay a fee. Only if you are investing a very small sum on a low-commission product will it be more worthwhile to opt for an adviser who earns commission rather than a fee.

IFAs are required by law to carry personal indemnity insurance that will protect you in the event of fraud.

For further information, IFA Promotions is on 0117 971 1177 and will supply a list of independent financial advisers in your area. The register of fee-based advisers is run by Money Management (0117 976 9444).

Advisers Who Recommend the Products of Only One Company

These include tied agents (these are agents of only one financial services/life insurance company and include organizations such as banks and building societies) and company representatives (financial advisers who work for or represent one company). These advisers must select the most suitable or appropriate product for your needs from the range offered by the company that employs them.

Who Offers Advice?

- banks

- building societies

- life insurance companies – their employees/company representatives and agents

- fund management groups

- independent financial advisers

- stockbrokers

- merchant banks (only for those with larger investment portfolios)

- accountants and solicitors

- insurance brokers

- a range of newer financial companies from high-street retailers such as Marks & Spencer to the likes of Virgin

EXPECTING THE UNEXPECTED

A "job for life" is a thing of the past and the Welfare State will only provide you with the flimsiest of safety nets in the future. We must all learn to be more entrepreneurial and self-reliant and the provision of a robust safety net is the key to your happiness and future peace of mind. **Nigel Farquharson Agencies Ltd (NFA)** has long foreseen this brave, new world and based its financial planning on a simple premise: always expect the unexpected!

NFA has the confidence in its own expertise to give **you** the confidence to face the financial future with equanimity – to know that whatever life throws at you, whether it is a golden opportunity or a rumbling dark cloud, you will have the resources to cope with a sure foot and an easy mind.

When you consult NFA, you are taking the first steps in drawing up a blueprint for a secure future: – a future born of confidence in yourself, confidence in your adviser and, above all, confidence in your financial ability to ride any storms. **NFA is the young professional's adviser for the entrepreneurial age!**

Picking an Investment Adviser

Personal recommendations can be useful. But remember that your friend/colleague/relative may have been seduced by clever sales patter, and it can often take years for them to realize that they have invested in a poor performing investment scheme. But if you know someone who has had a good ongoing relationship with an adviser then that is a recommendation worth pursuing.

Go to more than one adviser. There is nothing to stop you from taking advice from two or three to compare their recommendations.

If you are looking for a specific type of investment find a specialist. Some advisers concentrate on one type of investment, such as pensions or PEPs.

Do not be lazy and deal only with organizations that approach you or send you literature through the post. Be pro-active and seek out advice.

Evaluating an Investment Adviser

1   Check that the company is authorized by one of the regulatory organizations to carry on investment business. You can do this by telephoning the Securities and Investments Board central register on 0171 929 3652. You will also be able to find out if there has been any disciplinary action against the firm. Do not go ahead and sign anything until you have done this simple task. The SIB has a free booklet called *How to Spot the Investment Cowboys*; for a copy call 0171 638 1240.

2   Check if the financial adviser sells just one company's products or is independent and can select the most suitable investment from a range of companies.

3   Check the level of authorization as there are different
    categories. Some financial advisers are not authorized
    to handle clients' money, which means you must make
    your cheques payable to the investment company and
    not to the independent financial adviser.

4   Check what qualifications your adviser holds. All
    advisers must pass the financial planning certificate
    (FPC) exam (or its equivalent) but these are only the
    minimum qualifications. The initials MSFA, ACII or
    FCII signal higher qualifications.
        Watch out for impressive initials after a name – they
    may mean little. Member of the Institute of Financial
    Planning merely means the adviser has paid a sub-
    scription. Member of the Life Insurance Association
    by Diploma merely means the adviser has passed the
    basic FPC exam.

5   Find out how much experience the adviser has. You
    should ideally see someone with at least five years'
    experience if you want specialist financial advice.

6   Check that the adviser is competent (and authorized)
    to deal with all your financial needs, and ask if it will
    be necessary to bring in other specialists such as tax
    or pensions experts.

7   Find out how long the company for which the adviser
    works has been in business and how many clients it
    has.

8   Ask if you can speak to other clients of the firm to see
    how happy they are with the advice that they have
    been given.

9   Ask how the adviser will be renumerated. Fee-based advisers should rebate any commission paid by life insurance/financial services companies in full (this will be added to your investment). If the adviser works on a commission basis, ask if you will receive advice on products that do *not* pay commission.

10   Always choose an adviser you feel you can trust as you will have a better working relationship.

What Happens When You See a Financial Adviser?

So that you can be recommended the most appropriate products to suit your financial requirements, you should be asked about your financial and personal circumstances, what your needs are, what you are hoping to achieve from your investments, and a range of other information. This may seem an intrusion but this 'fact find' is essential.

Once the adviser has chosen an investment/pension he or she thinks meets your needs you should be given a 'key features' document describing the product and be told how much commission your adviser will earn – but only on the products recommended. So ask how the commission paid compares to other products and other types of investments.

The key features document will tell you:

The investment details: These will explain the policy terms, its risks and aims, your rights to cancel, what happens if you cannot pay a premium and other policy/investment details.

Charges: Once you have selected an investment you will be told how much is deducted in charges. But as you are only given this information after selecting a product it can make charges difficult to compare. For unit trusts and PEPs you will be told the specific charges, and for other products such as endowments and pensions you will also be told how much the charges will reduce your investment returns and how much they could total over the term of the policy.

How much you can expect to make: Advisers can only show how much you are likely to make on your investment using set percentage returns. This prevents them from giving you unrealistic projections of the amount you will receive. Remember that there is no guarantee that your investments will match these illustration rates.

The set illustration rates are:

> **Pensions:** 7 per cent, 9 per cent and 12 per cent, plus how much you will get back if you decide to transfer your pension before the end of the policy term (including the amounts in the first five years)

Endowments: 5 per cent, 7.5 per cent and 10 per cent, plus surrender values in the first five years and details of what you would get back if you cash the policy in before the end of the policy term

PEPs: 6 per cent, 9 per cent and 12 per cent, plus details of the charges

The adviser may also show you past-performance league tables to show you that the investment he or she is recommending is a top performing scheme. Once again, this is no guarantee to future performance. You should ask how this particular investment compares to others. For instance, if you are buying an endowment policy you may be shown the top performing with-profits fund, but how well does this compare to the top performing unit-linked fund?

What You Should Do Next?

Go away and think about any investment recommendations. Never sign anything on the spot and if you are pressurized into doing so question why the adviser is in such a hurry.

What Happens If You Are Not Happy With the Advice Given?

Cancellation Rights

If you feel that you were pressurized into making an investment decision or simply change your mind, you will normally be able to cancel the investment, provided that you do so within 14 days of signing. The exception to this rule is where you bought an investment on an 'execution only' basis, which means you received no financial advice.

Warning: If you agree to buy an investment on an 'execution only' basis – with no advice – you are taking responsibility for your own decisions, and if you have picked a poor performing investment, one with high charges or one that is not suitable, you have no protection under the Financial Services Act. Telephone-based financial services companies usually operate on a no-advice basis. As such, once you have agreed to buy an investment you may not be able to pull out of the agreement without losing some or all of your initial investment.

Complaints

All financial services companies must have a procedure to deal with complaints.

If you feel you have been badly advised or that the service offered by your company is poor, you must first complain to the company itself. Keep a copy of all correspondence and a note of all telephone conversations. Detail why you are not happy and what action you expect.

If you are not satisfied with the response and you think that the company has contravened the Financial Services Act, you can then take your complaint to the appropriate regulatory authority. Only after you have exhausted a company's in-house complaints procedure and if you want compensation can you then take your case to one of the ombudsmen. These are listed in Chapter 11.

6 *Investing*

You have to speculate if you want to accumulate.

Saving is essential to provide you with a safety net. But over the long-term – three to five years or more – the only way to make your money work for you is by investing.

Since the Second World war the average deposit account has halved in value once inflation has been taken into account. At the same time the average value of shares has multiplied a dozen times. If you bought and sold at the wrong time, you could have lost money on a share-based investment but, over the long-term, equities outperform savings. Even in 1987, when Black Monday led to a stock market crash, the major shares still rose in value over the year. The rule is short-term risk but long-term gain.

Remember that there is no such thing as a high return, low risk investment.

Before comparing different types of investment it is essential that you know what you hope to achieve by investing.

How Long are You Looking to Invest For?

Short-term

It is never a good idea to invest over the short-term unless you are planning to make a quick killing on a share tip or are cashing in a privatization or building society share offer.

In most cases the costs of investing mean that you have to invest for at least two to three years to make a profit.

Medium-term

If you are looking to invest over a period of three to seven years then you should consider PEPs (while they are still available), unit trusts, investment trusts, a share portfolio and open-ended investment companies.

Long-term

All the medium-term investments are also suitable over the longer term. In addition, ten-year (and longer term) life insurance linked investments can also be considered.

How Much Risk are You Prepared to Take?

Generally the higher the risk the higher the potential reward – and losses. This is known as the risk/reward ratio. Not all equity-linked investments carry a high risk. Some schemes have a built-in guarantee but you will usually have to pay for this in higher fees, penalties for early encashment of the investment or a potentially poorer – although safer – investment return.

Do You Want Income or Growth?

As a younger investor it is unlikely that you will want to invest for income. However, some income generating investments may still be a good investment if this income is reinvested. You will find that many investments produce either an income or growth and some produce both.

Do You Want to Invest a Regular Monthly Amount or a Lump Sum?

It is unlikely that you will have a lump sum unless you have a redundancy payment or inheritance. As such, regular investing is likely to be the only option and it can have its advantages as you can generally invest smaller sums (from around £30 to £50 a month) and regular investing helps to iron out fluctuations in the stock market.

Timing Investments

Although the stock market rises over the long term it does not do so at a steady rate. The ideal time to invest is when the market has dipped, as you can buy more shares for your money and have the potential for a greater gain. However, it is not easy to predict when this will be. Regular investing can work to your advantage thanks to 'pound-cost averaging'.

This takes the pressure off picking the best time to invest and works like this: when the stock market rises so does the value of your investments but you get less shares for your money; when it falls you buy more shares or units of investment for your money and have the potential for greater gains. So over the long run you make the most of rises and falls in the stock market.

The Investment Options

Shares

Minimum investment: Can be as low as £50 but you will find that the dealing costs (costs involved in buying and selling shares) eat into your investment making small share deals uneconomical.

Risk factors: It is safer to diversify in a portfolio of shares or in an investment fund to spread the risks rather than gambling on the performance of just one or two shares. If the company goes into liquidation you could lose all your investment.

Type of investor: A risk-taker who understands how the stock market works; those who receive free shares (either from a building society or their employer); and those who invest in privatizations which tend to be less risky as new share issues tend to be priced to encourage a wide take-up of shares and an instant profit is almost guaranteed.

Tax position: You must pay stamp duty of 0.5 per cent on all share purchases. Tax on dividends (the income you earn from shares) is deducted at 20 per cent before you receive your dividend payment. Only higher-rate (40 per cent) taxpayers need to pay more tax and must declare this on their tax return. A few investors may also be liable for capital gains tax (see Chapter 10 for more details). Share dividends and profits are tax-free if you buy them through a Personal Equity Plan (PEP) (see the section on PEPs later in this chapter).

What are shares?

Shares are issued by companies to raise finance and are just one type of equity. You will generally buy an 'ordinary share', which entitles you to some of the company's profits in the form of a dividend (usually paid twice a year), and will have a vote on major decisions that the company takes. The value of the shares can rise and fall with the fortunes of the company and is also affected by outside factors such as the state of the general economy and fluctuations in world stock markets.

The FTSE 100

Most smaller investors opt for shares in the FTSE (Financial Times Share Index) 100 top shares, which is known as the 'footsie'. This index lists the shares in the largest and, in theory, safest companies. The index rises in points so do not confuse these with percentage increases. There are also indices for the top 250 and 350 shares as well as for smaller companies.

The all-share index

Despite its name this index does not cover all shares listed on the London Stock Market – only 850 – but in terms of market capitalization (value of shares) it does cover around 96 per cent.

The Alternative Investment Market (AIM)

The Alternative Investment Market is more risky as it lists the shares of newer companies that have less of a trading history or smaller market value. This market runs on a matched basis, which means you may find it hard to sell your shares as a buyer must first be found.

Penny shares

These are – as their name implies – shares that you can buy for just a few pence each. Again, the risks can be high but a 1p increase in a 1p share will double your money – a difficult feat to achieve with a major share. *The Penny Share Guide*, a monthly subscription newsletter, is available by ringing 0171 447 4040.

Dividends

This is the income you earn from your shares and is a portion of the company's profits. The gross dividend (before tax is deducted) divided by the share price is known as the yield.

The half-year payment is known as the 'interim' dividend, and the end of year payment as the 'final' dividend. In addition to this income you should also expect your shares to rise in value.

Not all dividends are in the form of a cash payment. 'Scrip' dividends offer investors additional shares and these are often worth much more than the cash. For tax purposes, scrip dividends are treated the same as other dividends.

Finding out how well a share performs

To find out how well a share is performing you can look at its performance over the last year in the share pages of newspapers. This will show you the highest and lowest values that the share has reached. The other way of judging a share is by the price/earnings ratio, also known as the p/e. This is the share price divided by the earnings per share. It shows you how many years it would take the company to earn enough in profits to match the share price. So if the share price is 500p and the earnings per share are 50p then it has a p/e ratio of 10 (500/50 = 10).

A low p/e ratio means that the share is cheap in relation to the company's earnings potential. It can mean that the company has a stable outlook. However, more often it means that the share price is low because its prospects are poor.

A high p/e ratio can mean that the share is in great demand but sometimes it is high because earnings are low.

How to pick a share

Sectors: Shares are split into sectors depending on the type of business. For example, there are sectors for consumer goods, utilities, general industrials, and consumer goods. Monitoring a sector's performance can give an indication of the future prospects of a particular share within that sector. However, not all shares perform as well as the sector.

Share tips: The financial pages of newspapers, including *The Daily Telegraph* give investment tips and select shares that are worth considering as investments.

Stockbroker reports: Generally you have to be a private client with a large portfolio of investments and pay a fee to benefit from a stockbroker's advice. However, some stock-brokers and investment advisers do issue investment reports for those with smaller amounts to invest. You can also monitor stockbrokers' advice by reading the financial pages of news-papers.

Company information: Once you are a shareholder you should be sent an annual report by the company in which you hold shares. It details the financial accounts of the company and gives a summary of its activities and plans for the future. As a holder of ordinary voting shares in a company you can also attend the Annual General Meeting at which the senior management give details about the future prospects of the company.

The cost of buying and selling shares

Dealing costs can be as low as £12 or £15 for smaller share deals, and a percentage of 0.75 per cent for larger share deals up to a maximum of £60. Postal and telephone services are often the cheapest. Do not forget stamp duty of 0.5 per cent on share purchases.

The bid-offer spread

When you look in the newspaper for the value of a share you will see the mid-price at the time of the stock market closing the day before. So remember that this price is likely to have changed.

There are in fact two prices of each share – the price you pay, or offer price and the price you receive when you sell a share, or bid price. Shares in smaller companies have a bigger bid-offer spread but in general it is no more than a few per cent. This spread also applies to other types of share-based investments, such as unit trusts and investment trusts. It means that if you buy and sell shares at the same price you will get less back than you paid even though the price appears to be identical.

Different types of share services

Execution-only: This means that you take full responsibility for any investment decisions as you receive no advice. Execution-only share dealing is far cheaper that other share dealing services and is most commonly used by those who want to sell small shareholdings such as shares in privatized companies.

Discretionary: This means that all investment decisions are at the discretion of your adviser, although he or she will work within investment guidelines agreed with you. This type of service is normally restricted to those wanting portfolio management and is the most expensive.

Advisory: This simply means that you have complete control over investment decisions but you take advice from your stockbroker or financial adviser.

Shareholder perks

In some cases it can be worth buying shares just to receive the perks on offer, such as discounts or free offers, as in some cases the freebies are worth more than the shares. In most cases there is no minimum shareholding.

Some of the perks on offer include:

- £1 off your bill if you spend more than £5 at Boots

- 20 per cent off Jaeger clothes

- a free meal for two and a free bottle of wine from the restaurant chain Chez Gerard

- 10 to 20 per cent off food and accommodation at Hilton Hotels

- 10 per cent discounts on Airtours holidays

- a 15 per cent discount card for Austin Reed shops

- 50 per cent discount on PEP charges at Bank of Scotland

- discount vouchers at Iceland Group shops

- 25 per cent discount card at Sketchley

- 10 per cent discount at Storehouse shops

- 10 per cent discount at the Savoy Group of hotels and restaurants

- up to £3000 off a new home built by Bellway

These are correct at the time of writing. Minimum share-holdings vary from just one share to a minimum of 3000.

Financial advisers Hargreaves Lansdown produce a guide entitled '*Attractive Perks for UK Shareholders*' (0800 850 661) and your stockbroker will probably have a list.

Settlement

This is the process of dealing with the paperwork and payments. If you hold share certificates (proving your ownership of the shares) in your own name, settlement usually takes ten days.

To cut down on paperwork, costs and settlement times stockbrokers are increasingly asking that shares are held in a nominee account. This means you will not hold the share certificates. Shares are registered in the name of the nominee account but you still remain the beneficial owner and must pay tax. But check with your broker that you will still receive shareholder information and that you are not losing out on any shareholder perks. There will be a fee for this service.

If you are planning to deal in shares regularly you can, for an extra £20, become a sponsored member of the Stock Exchange electronic settlement system, Crest, which has a five-day settlement period. Shares are registered in your name and you do not need share certificates in order to sell shares.

Call the Stock Exchange publications request line on 0171 797 1372 for booklets on share ownership and being a shareholder.

Share and investment clubs

If you really want to take investing seriously and want to share information with other shareholders you can join an investment club. These usually meet once a month. ProShare (0171 600 6365) gives information on share ownership and share clubs and the National Federation of Investment Clubs (0171 394 5200) and can supply you with a list of existing clubs.

Finding a stockbroker

Many banks and building societies offer instant share dealing services and there are several low-cost telephone dealing services. Or you can go to a stockbroker. ProShare, the organization set up to promote share ownership, has several booklets, including a guide to brokers who specialize in new share issues. Write to ProShare, Library Chambers, 13–14 Basinghall Street, London, EC2V 5BQ or telephone 0171 600 6365.

The Association of Private Client Investment Managers and Stockbrokers (0171 247 7080) produces a list of private client stockbrokers.

Other Ways to Invest in the Stock Market

Most other types of equity market investments including corporate bonds, preference shares, permanent interest-bearing shares (issued by building societies), and debentures pay a fixed rate of interest or dividends, and as such may not be suitable for younger investors looking for growth rather than income.

Warrants give you the right to buy and sell a share in a company at future-set dates with the price fixed from the outset. You are therefore gambling that the share price will rise to above the set (excerise) price. If it falls you are under no obligation to buy the share. Warrants can be traded on the stock market and as such you can buy them with no intention of taking up the rights to buy the share. Warrants are generally priced below that of the related share. No income is paid.

Futures and options

These are known as derivatives and are much more risky than shares, although they can also be used to reduce the risks of investing. You can take out an option that the share index will fall so that you gain even if the value of your shares falls. This is known as hedging – as in hedging your bets. You can also bet on individual shares rising or falling.

The reason why futures and options are riskier than shares is gearing – only a small proportion of the investment is paid for. So if you pay £1000 on a £10,000 contract and the price increases by 10 per cent you would double your money making a further £1000. However, if the price falls by 20 per cent you will not only lose your original investment of £1000 but must pay a further £1000 to cover these losses. With shares you can only lose your investment.

There are now unit trusts that invest in futures and options to hedge investment risks and to help the funds match the performance of the stock market.

Gilts

These are British Government stocks or gilt-edged securities. They are a way for the Government to borrow money. However, they are unlikely to appeal to younger investors as they are aimed at those wanting income rather than growth.

Pooled Investments

As discussed above, investing in just one or two shares carries a higher risk and the costs can be high if you are investing a small sum. A safer and usually cheaper way to invest in the stock market is through collective investments. These pool money from a large number of investors, allowing the fund manager to invest in a more diversified range of investments.

Collective investments include unit trusts, investment trusts, open-ended investment companies, and offshore funds.

Unit trusts

Minimum investment: Can be as low as £20 or £30 a month or £500 for a lump sum, although in some cases this is lower.

Risk factors: The value of shares can rise as well as fall so there is always a risk. But the spread of investments should make these safer than investing in just one or two shares. Some unit-trust plans now offer a guaranteed minimum return to reduce the risk of losses.

Type of investor: Anyone wanting to invest in the stock market for three to five years, who is prepared to take some risks and who does not want to invest for a fixed term (unit trusts can be sold at any time).

Tax position: Unit trusts are tax free provided you invest using a Personal Equity Plan. Otherwise income tax will be deducted before dividend income is paid at 20 per cent (this tax credit will fall to 10 per cent in 1999). Currently only higher rate taxpayers must pay additional tax to bring this up to 40 per cent. A few investors may also be liable to capital gains tax (see Chapter 10).

What are unit trusts?

These are collective investments – savers' money is pooled and then invested by a fund manager. This fund is divided into units of equal value (your investment is used to buy a number of these units) and the value of these units is revalued every day to reflect the rises and falls in the underlying investments.

Unit trusts are very popular with more than £130 billion invested and some 8 million unitholder accounts.

Performance varies widely. For instance, in 1996 the top performing fund grew by over 50 per cent in just 12 months, with the average for UK growth funds being 9.5 per cent.

This looks quite impressive until you compare the gain with the FTSE All-Share Index, which rose by 17.39 per cent. If you were unlucky to pick the bottom performing fund almost half the value of your investment would have been wiped out.

Remember, past performance is no guarantee of future performance.

How long do I have to invest for?

There is no minimum investment period and you can cash in your units whenever you want. However, the costs you pay to invest (generally between 5 and 6 per cent of your initial investment) will usually mean that you will need to invest for at least three years to make a reasonable profit.

Can I change the amount I invest?

Unlike life-insurance based investments, you can vary the amount you invest, stop investing and pay in additional lump sums or withdraw part of your investment at any time – usually with no financial penalties.

What do unit trusts invest in?

There are over 1600 unit trusts on offer and this includes a vast range of investments. There is even a Football Fund that invests in shares of UK and Continental football clubs. Unit trusts mainly invest in shares but can also invest in cash, bonds, gilts, and even other funds.

Unit trusts are split into sectors with the most popular being:

- UK growth

- UK income

- UK income & growth

- UK smaller companies

- UK gilt & fixed interest

- UK equity & bond

- Tracker or index trusts (which aim to match the performance of the FTSE 100 or other share index)

- Fund of funds (which invest in a range of unit trust funds)

- Cash funds (these have lower charges and can be switched into if you want to reduce your exposure to the stockmarket)

- International funds (which can either invest in a particular country or in a geographical region)

You can also invest in an ethical fund which does not invest in companies in the arms, tobacco, alcohol or gambling business.

Tracker/index trusts

Although the main attraction of unit trusts (and other pooled investments) is that a professional fund manager makes all the investment decisions on your behalf, you may be shocked to hear that many underperform the stock market as a whole.

This has led to the innovation of tracker funds, which aim to match the movement in the stock market – usually the growth of the FTSE 100 Index. Charges are often much lower than for other unit trusts. There are are two potential drawbacks: firstly, charges mean that the fund may slightly underperform the stock market; and secondly, the fund is not actively managed so if shares fall dramatically the fund manager will not be able to change investment strategy and switch to cash investments to minimize losses. However, these funds do offer investors the safety of knowing that they will not be investing in a fund that significantly under-performs, and tend to offer better returns than many other unit trusts.

Different types of units

Unit trusts can offer 'accumulation' or growth units and 'distribution' or income units, which pay out an income quarterly, twice a year, or annually. Most younger investors will be interested in the former. Any income, such as dividends and interest, earned by the trust is reinvested and as such this helps to boost performance.

If you invest in accumulation units you will have to pay tax on the income that has been reinvested if you are a higher rate taxpayer (unless you invest via a PEP). The fund manager will send you an annual statement.

What are the charges?

There are two charges:

1   The initial charge, which is a percentage – usually between 4 and 6 per cent – of what you invest. This is deducted at the time of investment.

Intense competition between fund managers, particularly in the PEP market, means that some unit trusts now have no initial charge.

2   The annual management charge is a deduction of between 1 and 2 per cent of the amount invested. This is deducted annually, usually from the trust's income.

Pricing – the hidden costs

If you look at unit trust prices in the newspaper you will see two prices – the selling or cancellation price (what you get when you sell your units), and the buying or creation price (what you pay for the shares). Generally you receive around 5 or 7 per cent less for your units than the price you paid for them, although this spread can be as much as 10 or 11 per cent.

There are times when this spread of prices varies. When a trust is in demand quoted prices are at the top end of the range. In this case the trust will be on an 'offer basis'. Conversely, when more unitholders are selling than buying, shares may have to be sold to meet redemptions and the price given to sellers will be lower.

When you come to sell you will probably find that your fund manager deals on a 'forward pricing' basis, which means that any purchases or sales will be at the price set on the next valuation. In some cases pricing may be on an 'historic' basis, which means that the price is that set at the most recent valuation (the one usually quoted in newspapers).

Discounts on charges

When you invest in a unit trust your financial adviser will usually receive commission. Even if you buy direct from the fund manager you will still have to pay these costs, as unit trust managers charge the same regardless of whether you receive advice or not.

However, some fund managers reduce charges if you invest directly during an offer period while a new fund is being launched, and some discount and fee basis advisers will rebate part or all of the commission they are paid.

Switching investments

If you are unhappy with the performance of the funds you have selected you can switch to another fund managed by the same company and usually the initial charges will be reduced, although some fund managers do allow a certain number of free switches.

If you want to switch to another fund management group you will have to pay the full initial charge. So switching could cost you between 5 and 6 per cent of your investment. As such, you should be sure that the performance of the new fund will more than make up for these costs. However, some fund managers will offer a discount so the costs can be cut to between 1 and 4 per cent.

Also remember that if you sell your units – even to switch them to another fund – you could be liable for capital gains tax and will lose out because of the bid-offer spread.

Switching other investments into unit trusts

Many unit trust groups offer share exchange schemes that allow investors to sell shares and use the money raised to invest in a unit trust, usually with a discount on the charges.

How to buy unit trusts

You can either buy through a financial intermediary such as a bank or building society, an independent financial adviser, or a stockbroker, or you can deal directly with a unit trust group by phone, by post, or by responding to advertisements in newspapers or magazines.

Monitoring the performance of your unit trust

The value of the trust is usually revalued every day and as such the value of units can rise and fall on a daily basis. These prices are quoted daily in the newspapers, including the _Daily Telegraph_ and _Sunday Telegraph_. These list the buying and selling prices.

How to find out more

The Association of Unit Trusts and Investment Funds (AUTIF) runs the Unit Trust Information Service. Telephone 0181 207 1361.

Investment trusts

Minimum investment: Can be as low as £20 or £30 a month or £250 for a lump sum.

Risk factors: The value of shares can rise as well as fall so there is always a risk. But the spread of investments should make these safter than investing in just one or two shares. Investment trust performance tends to be slightly more volatile than unit trusts.

Type of investor: Anyone wanting to invest in the stock-market for three to five years, who is prepared to take some risks and who does not want to invest for a fixed term – like shares, investment trust holdings can be sold at any time.

Tax position: Investment trusts are tax free provided you invest using a Personal Equity Plan. Otherwise income tax will be deducted before dividend income is paid at 20 per cent (set to fall to 10 per cent in 1999). Currently only higher rate taxpayers must pay additional tax to bring this up to 40 per cent. You may also be liable to capital gains tax.

What are investment trusts?

Despite their name these are not trusts. They are investment companies quoted on the Stock Exchange. Like unit trusts they pool investors' money and then invest this in a range of investments including shares, fixed-interest securities, property, and even other investment trusts. But instead of buying units (as with unit trusts) you buy shares in the company. There are more than three hundred quoted on the stock market and they look after nearly £60 billion of capital on behalf of investors.

Investment trusts are close-ended investments, which means they have a fixed number of shares. Unit trusts on the other hand are open-ended, so the number of units can rise or fall depending on demand.

How long do I need to invest for?

Generally, you should look to invest for three to five years to cover the cost of investing and make a reasonable profit. However, if your investment trust performance does well or if you need all or part of your money, you can sell your investment trust shares at any time.

How investment trusts are priced

Investment trusts are valued very differently from unit trusts. The value of investment trust shares moves in a similar way to all shares that are affected by the general economy, movements in the stockmarket, and demand for the shares.

The value of a unit trust unit rises and falls in line with the value of the underlying investment fund. However, the total value of investment trust shares can be greater or less than the value of the assets held by the investment trust.

If the total value of the investment trust shares quoted on the stock market is £500,000, and the value of all the investments held by the investment trust is greater than £550,000, then you are buying these investments at a 'discount'. If you buy investment trust shares at a discount and they move upwards you have a greater potential for profits.

Likewise, if the investment trust share is in demand then the value of the underlying investments can be greater than the total worth of all the investment trust shares. You are then paying a 'premium'. If the investment trust shares then move to a discount, you will lose.

Most investment trusts trade at a discount of around 9 per cent (although this can vary). This adds an extra element of risk to investing in investment trusts.

What can they invest in?

Investment trusts can invest in a wider range of investments than unit trusts. However, this also makes them less easy to categorize. There are some twenty different sectors but in general the investment scope is more broadly defined than for unit trusts and as such performance can vary widely within each trust sector. Trusts can either aim for capital growth or income, although half are general trusts offering a mixture of both.

Investment trusts must distribute at least 85 per cent of their investment income to shareholders and cannot hold more than 15 per cent of their assets in any one share. The usual number of shareholdings is between forty and two hundred.

The fact that investment trusts are 'closed' investments means that when markets are rising there is no new money to buy more shares to take advantage of rising share values. So unlike unit trusts, investment trusts can borrow money to invest. This is known as gearing and adds an extra element of risk to investment trusts.

What are the charges?

There is often no initial charge but some trusts do make a charge of up to 5 per cent if you buy the shares through a PEP.

There will be a difference or 'spread' between the offer (buying) and bid (selling) prices.

If you buy through a stockbroker, bank, building society or other share dealing service there will be a dealing charge that for smaller sums can be disproportionately high because of minimum dealing charges. The cheaper way to invest is through a savings scheme run by the investment trust that accepts regular and one-off investments (but not all investment trusts offer this option). This will have charges – either an annual management charge or a purchase and sale charge. These charges are far lower than for unit trusts and range from nothing to 4 per cent.

As with other share purchases you must pay 0.5 per cent stamp duty.

Switching other investments into an investment trust

Several companies offer a share exchange service to enable you to swap holdings of other shares for investment trust shares with the dealing costs reduced.

Different types of investment trust share

In some cases you do not just buy a simple ordinary share in an investment trust, as there are several types on offer. These trusts are known as split capital trusts and are designed to cater for different investment needs, such as those seeking high income and low capital growth and those wanting high capital growth but no income.

In addition there can be other types of shares that make investment trusts slightly more complicated than unit trusts.

Zero dividend preference shares give no income at all – hence the term 'zero dividend'. These shares also have a fixed redemption date, although they can be bought and sold at any time. Stepped preference shares offer a combination of income and capital returns with a fixed redemption value and a fixed rate of annual dividend growth.

You can also buy investment trust warrants – the right to buy a share at a fixed price at a later date (see the section on shares) – but these can be high risk. In 1983 they produced average returns of 180 per cent but since then the situation has reversed and some have fallen almost 100 per cent in the last year.

Where can I buy investment trusts?

Investment trusts can be bought through a stockbroker, a bank or building society that offers a sharedealing service, and financial intermediaries. When a new trust is launched the company will publish a prospectus and this will appear in at least one newspaper with a coupon to apply for shares. Or you can buy directly from the company using a savings scheme.

Monitoring performance

As with other shares, investment trust prices are published daily in the newspapers.

How to find out more

The Association of Investment Trust Companies (AITC) has an enquiry line (0171 431 5222) for further information and free leaflets about investment trusts.

Investment trusts versus unit trusts

The top performing investment trusts tend to outperform the best performing unit trust. However, there is a bigger spread of performance, with the worst performing investment trust producing bigger losses than the poorest unit trust. On average, investment trusts perform better than unit trusts partly because of the lower charges. But be prepared for more volatility. (See Table 1.)

Offshore Trusts

These are investment funds run from offshore tax havens. Although these can include exotic locations such as Bermuda, in most cases these funds are run from Jersey, Guernsey, the Isle of Man and Luxembourg. When buying an offshore investment it is safer to pick a country that regulates its funds. Those in the European Union can apply to be a UCITS (Undertaking for Collective Investment in Transferable Securities) fund.

You may think that an offshore fund operated from a tax haven would be tax free. However, all income is liable to income tax. There are two types of fund: 'distributor' funds, which pay out most of the income to investors, and 'non-distributor' funds, in which income is reinvested. However, non-distributor fund profits are taxed as income, not capital gains. So if you have one of these accumulator funds you cannot escape tax by setting off profits against your annual capital gains tax allowance of £6500 (the 1997–98 threshold). Generally, you will be better off opting for an investment that is liable to capital gains tax because most taxpayers do not use up their annual allowance.

Table 1: Past performance of Unit Trusts and Investment Trusts

£1000 invested (offer to bid) up to 30 June 1997 with income reinvested compared to a £1000 investment in shares and a savings account

Investment type	5 years	10 years
Unit Trusts		
UK growth funds	£1,906.06	£2,047.78
UK growth & income	£1,883.05	£2,217.71
UK smaller companies	£1,887.01	£1,713.43
UK equity income	£1,894.06	£2,211.88
International growth	£2,032.40	£2,212.55
Indices funds	£2,148.36	£2,772.41
Investment Trusts		
UK general	£1,969.80	£2,262.33
UK capital growth	£1,949.66	£1,569.30
UK smaller companies	£1,714.58	£1,577.48
UK income & growth	£1,938.30	£2,605.98
International capital growth	£2,298.29	£2,555.33
Shares		
FTSE 100	£2,174.38	£2,869.80
FT All-Share Index	£2,122.35	£2,675.02
Savings		
90-day notice account	£1,200.52	£1,816.65
30-day notice account £500 invested	£1,170.07	£1,732.38

Source: The Association of Unit Trusts and Investment Funds and The Association of Investment Trust companies

Personal Equity Plans (PEPs)

Minimum investment: Can be as low as £25 or £30 a month or from £500 for a lump sum.

Risk factors: These can vary depending on the underlying investment – either shares, unit trusts, or investment trusts. Some PEPs have guaranteed returns.

Type of investor: Anyone who is aged 18 and over and a UK resident can open a PEP. The costs of investing mean that they are generally a better option for higher rate taxpayers than for lower rate taxpayers. Basic rate taxpayers only gain if the tax saving on dividends outweighs the extra charges. As fewer than 1 per cent of taxpayers pay capital gains tax, this tax break is not worth paying for.

Tax position: PEPs are currently free of income and capital gains tax – but only until 1999 so make the most of the tax breaks while you can.

What are PEPs?

These allow you to invest in shares, unit trusts and investment trusts free of tax. Currently, PEP funds can reclaim the 20 per cent tax that is deducted from share dividends. However, this tax break will no longer be available after 5 April 1999 when PEPs will be superseded by the new Individual Savings Account. Do not let this deter you from investing, as you will be able to switch your PEP investments into the new account. At the time of writing the exact details of the new ISA have yet to be finalized but it will have tax breaks.

If you had invested the maximum allowed since PEPs were first launched ten years ago, you would have invested some £78,000 of capital free of tax that would be worth more than £100,000.

A £1000 investment in the average unit trust PEP over the last five years would be worth £1990 (at the time of writing) compared to just £1235 in a good ninety-day savings account. Over the past five years, the top performing investment trust PEP has turned £1000 into £4267, and the top performing unit trust PEP has turned £1000 into £3380.

Increasing competition among PEP providers has kept charges low and they are becoming safer, with funds that offer a guaranteed rate of return and tracker funds that track the performance of the stock market.

There are more than one thousand different PEPs on offer from more than two hundred plan managers. The main features of PEPs have been covered in the sections on shares, unit and investment trusts. PEPs can be bought directly through the PEP manager or through a financial adviser or stockbroker.

Should I invest in a PEP?

A PEP is not an investment but a means of investing tax free. However, you should not be seduced by the tax breaks as the savings do not always outweigh the costs.

For instance, if you were to receive a windfall of £1400 shares from a converting building society and earned £56 in dividends, as a basic rate taxpayer you would pay £11.20 in tax (tax on dividends is deducted at 20 per cent).

However, if you were to invest in a PEP – even one with no initial fee but an annual charge – you could pay between £14 and £25 a year in charges. This is far more than the £11.20 a year you would save in tax.

But if you are a higher rate taxpayer you would be liable to £22.40 in tax on your dividend and will probably gain by investing in a PEP.

If you are planning to invest in a unit trust you may find that there are no extra charges for holding these units in a PEP, so even if you are a basic rate taxpayer you will gain.

Higher rate taxpayers and those likely to exceed the annual capital gains tax threshold (£6500 for 1997–98) will nearly always gain more in tax savings than they will pay in extra charges.

Always evaluate the underlying investment as well as any tax savings, and ask yourself if you would still invest in a particular unit trust, investment trust or share if you had to pay tax.

The PEP rules

▪ You can invest up to £6000 in every tax year (which runs from 6 April to 5 April) in a 'general PEP', which can be invested in a portfolio of shares, unit trusts, investment trusts, corporate bonds, or even in one just one share.

▪ In addition, up to £3000 can be invested in a 'single-company PEP', which invests in one company's shares.

▪ You can only invest in one general PEP and one single-company PEP in each tax year, but you do not have to buy them from the same PEP provider.

▪ Corporate PEPs are offered to employees and other investors who want to hold a single company's shares in a PEP (and often other shares or investment funds as well). These are general PEPs with the £6000 investing limit and if you have a corporate PEP you cannot invest in a general PEP in the same tax year. Although corporate PEPs are offered by companies quoted on the Stock Exchange they are administerd by authorized PEP managers.

▪ If you do not use up your PEP allowance you *cannot* carry it forward to the next year.

▓ All investments must be through an authorized PEP plan manager approved by the Inland Revenue. These include unit trust groups, investment trust companies, banks, building societies, insurance companies, stockbrokers and other financial advisers.

▓ PEPs _do not_ have to be disclosed on your Tax Return.

Warning: You can sell part of your PEP if you need to, but remember that this decision is irrevocable and you cannot then reinvest if that means you will exceed the total investment limits in a tax year.

What do PEPs invest in?

PEPs can be used to invest directly in shares or in the stock market using a pooled investment scheme such as a unit trust or an investment trust. You can either select your own shares or get a manager to run your PEP porfolio for you.

Eligible investments include ordinary shares of UK companies quoted on the Stock Exchange, shares of European Community companies listed on an EU stock exchange, corporate bonds, preference shares, and convertibles of UK and EU non-financial companies (but not corporate bonds of banks and building societies).

To qualify, pooled investments such as unit trusts and investment trusts must have at least 50 per cent of their assets invested either in UK or EU stock markets or in the securities listed above. Shares listed on the Alternative Investment Market are not eligible.

PEPs can also invest in cash deposits while the fund manager waits for the ideal time to invest in securities. However, cash deposits held in single-company PEPs must be invested within 42 days.

Up to £1500 can be invested in 'non-qualifying' funds that invest more than 50 per cent of their portfolio in shares quoted on other stock markets recognized by the Inland Revenue. This is worth considering by those wanting to diversify into overseas markets such as the US, Japan and the emerging economies. There is an added risk to investing overseas – exchange fluctuations.

Single-company PEPs cannot be used to invest in shares of investment trusts, even though these are publicly quoted companies. They are classed as pooled investments.

Transfering other investments into a PEP

Up to £3000 of shares acquired through an approved employee share option scheme or profit-sharing scheme can be transferred into a single company PEP without capital gains tax implications.

You can also transfer newly issued shares, including shares from privatizations and building society conversions, into a general or single company PEP, provided that this is done within 42 days of the allocation of the shares.

In other cases you will have to sell your existing investments. However, you can save on costs by using a share exchange scheme, which reduces the charges provided that the proceeds are invested in a unit trust or investment trust PEP.

Different types of PEPs

Managed PEPs: In these cases the investment decisions are made for you either by a unit trust or investment trust manager or by another fund manager such as a stockbroker. Alternatively, your investment adviser may manage your PEP by picking a selection of funds to meet your investment needs.

Some PEP managers offer a portfolio of shares rather than a collective investment. This is known as a discretionary fund management service. Some single-company PEPs also offer a 'managed' option, with the fund manager selecting a share for investment each year.

Tracker funds: These track the performance of the stock market. However very few funds actually track the FT All-Share Index. Most track the FTSE 100 index of the top 100 shares. Competition has brought charges down and good performance has made these relatively new funds increasingly popular. There is seldom any initial charge and annual management fees do not normally exceed 1 per cent.

£ CASH TIP £

Most fund managers fail to match consistently the performance of the FTSE 100 index. So a tracker fund will often give you better performance and the charges are far lower than for many other PEPs.

Guaranteed PEPs: These guarantee a minimum rate of return but tend to have higher charges. They are often only available for a limited period and guarantee the return of either all or most of your capital, regardless of stock market falls. In most cases you can still receive the full value of any rises in the stock market. But read the small print carefully and note that charges can be higher than for other PEPs.

Self-Select PEPs: These are exactly that – PEPs that enable you to select the investment yourself. The investments can either be shares, unit trusts, or investment trusts, and minimum investments are usually £250 upwards. The most important charge to be aware of is the dealing charge. If you are buying and selling small amounts on a regular basis and there is a minimum charge of say £50, you are likely to find that the dealing costs significantly eat into any profits you make and the £6000 investment limit may mean you cannot spread the risks of investing by picking a wide range of shares. To reduce the risks investors can chose to select their own range of managed funds and mix these with bonds and shares. However, managed funds will have higher charges of around 5 to 6 per cent of the initial investment and an annual management fee. As a result, these PEPs are more suitable for those with larger sums to invest and who have experience in selecting shares.

Always check how quickly the plan manager will react to your dealing instructions, as any delay can eat into profits you make. Some fund managers restrict the shares that can be bought to just the FTSE 100 or the All-Share Index.

Corporate Bond PEPs: Corporate bond PEPs invest in fixed-interest securites issued by UK and EU-based companies, and are increasingly popular as they offer a high and fixed income of usually over 8 per cent gross that is tax free. However, as their main appeal is to those wanting income rather than capital growth they are probably not suitable for younger investors.

Selecting a PEP

The things to compare are consistent (rather than just recent) good past performance of the fund manager and a particular fund – probably a UK growth fund, tracker fund, or another investment offering the potential for capital growth. You can check unit trust and investment trust prices daily in *The Daily Telegraph*. Newspapers also publish regular PEP performance league tables. Always look for consistent performance rather than just picking the PEP at the top of the most recent performance table. Then you should compare charges.

Once you have decided on a PEP manager you will then normally be given a choice of funds to invest in. Unit trust, investment trust and other PEP managers usually offer a range of funds with different levels of risk and different investment aims.

You can split your investments between these different funds or invest in just one.

What are the costs?

With a PEP that invests in a unit trust you will pay initial charges of up to 5 or 6 per cent of the amount you invest, and then an annual management fee of between 0.75 and 1.5 per cent. This means that if you cash in your PEP within the first few months you are likely to get back less than you invested unless investment returns have been exceptionally good.

PEPs that invest in investment trusts tend to have lower charges than unit trusts, with some having no initial charge and others a flat fee instead of a percentage charge. On smaller investments this flat fee can work out to be a very high percentage.

Charges on corporate PEPs are among the lowest, with several having no initial charge and an annual administration charge of around 0.5 to 1 per cent. However, some still charge up to 6 per cent. Single-company PEPs charge an annual fee of between 0.5 and 1 per cent and some PEP providers also levy an initial charge of either 0.5 to 1 per cent or between £10 and £50.

Remember that with all shares, unit trusts and investment trusts there is a difference between the buying price and selling price – this will also reduce your investment returns.

To cut costs it is possible to go to a discount broker who will refund some or all of the intitial commission paid to financial advisers. These direct PEP selling companies usually make a charge – say £25 – that on larger investments is often lower than the commission you are refunded.

£ CASH TIP £

Do not evaluate charges in isolation. Remember that it will be better to pay a 1.5 per cent management charge on a 7 per cent return than a 0.5 per cent charge on a 5 per cent return.

What if I am not happy with my PEP's performance?

Although you are only allowed to have one PEP in each financial year, if you are unhappy with the performance of your PEP you can either switch to a different fund managed by the same PEP provider or to a different PEP provider.

If you are switching to a fund run by the same PEP manager, charges are often reduced, however you will lose out on the bid/offer spread.

If you are switching your PEP to another PEP provider you will have to pay a new initial charge, will lose out on the bid/offer spread, may also be charged an exit fee, and will have to pay between £30 to £50 for the transfer.

You must follow the correct proceedure and must not cash in one PEP to invest in another. The new PEP manager must execute the transfer. You can also transfer PEP investments accumulated in previous years. In some cases you may find it difficult to transfer just one year's PEP investment, as PEPs bought in different years tend to be administered as one investment. Transfers usually take two to four weeks and your money should remain invested for all bar four or five days.

Warning: If you pay for your PEP by direct debit and want to switch PEPs at the end of the year, make sure that you cancel your direct debit. If after the start of the new tax year on 6 April you invest in your existing PEP, you will not be able to start another PEP as investors are only allowed to invest in one PEP each year.

How to find out more

Investment advisers Chase de Vere (0171 404 5766) publish a PEP guide that lists the one thousand plus PEPs currently on offer from over two hundred managers.

The Association of Unit Trusts and Investment Funds and the Association of Investment Trust Companies can also supply information (details are listed earlier in this chapter).

On the second Saturday of every month, _The Daily Telegraph_ publishes a performance table covering all the major unit trusts and investment trusts PEPs.

Open-ended Investment Companies

It is estimated that half of all unit trusts will convert into this new type of collective investment in the next few years. At the time of writing, only one had been launched and a few were in the pipeline. But, as they are expected to be increasingly popular, this is how they work.

OEICs are very similar to unit trusts. They are both 'open-ended', which means that the size of the fund can go up and down to reflect the amount invested. Investment trusts, on the other hand, are closed schemes, which means they have a fixed number of shares.

However, like investment trusts, OEICs are companies listed on the stock market so the price of the shares can rise and fall. But unlike investment trusts they will not trade at a premium or a discount to the assets.

OEICs have single pricing that means that they do not have separate buying and selling prices. They can be umbrella funds, which means that investors can switch from sub-fund to sub-fund within the OEICs for a lower charge than would be currently paid with a unit trust.

OEICs can only invest in certain share-based funds but there are proposals to extend the range to include cash and bond funds.

Unlike unit trusts, OEICS allow managers to set different charges for different types of investors and different amounts of investments. So if you buy direct from the fund manager you may not have to pay as much as an investor whose financial adviser is paid commission, and larger investors may benefit from lower charges.

Investment Bonds

These are investments offered by life insurance companies. Many require investors to invest for a minimum period, with financial penalties charged for early encashment of the policy. Some of your money will pay for a small amount of life insurance cover. Although the proceeds of these policies are tax free, these are not tax-free investments, as the life insurance company has already paid tax on the underlying investments, and you cannot reclaim this.

If you are buying a bond ask how charges, performance, flexibility and the commission paid to the adviser compare to PEPs, unit trusts and investment trusts.

Single-premium investment bonds

You will need to invest a lump sum of around £1000 minimum. Like unit trusts and other collective investments you can invest your money in a choice of funds. Your money is invested in one or more life insurance funds (there is usually a wide choice of funds and switching between these is cheaper than for unit trusts) and a small amount of your investment is used to buy a minimum amount of life insurance (usually slightly more than the value of the investment). There is a slight tax advantage for higher rate taxpayers seeking income but this tax break is being reviewed.

Regular premium investment plans

These are mainly Maximum Investment Plans, which have the minimum amount of life cover so most of your money is invested. You can invest from £50 a month upwards and usually need to invest for at least ten years, so if you can no longer afford your premiums or want to cash in your policy before the term is up you will lose out as surrender penalties will be charged. If you hold your policy for the full term, the final pay out is tax free. Over the ten years up to March 1997, a male non-smoker (aged thirty next birthday at the time of taking out the policy) who invested £50 a month would have invested £6000 and received at the end of the policy an average of almost £11,000, according to a survey by _Money Management_ magazine.

If you cash in the policy before ten years you can still take the proceeds without paying tax, provided you have been paying regular premiums for at least three-quarters of the term of the policy.

Guaranteed equity bonds

These guarantee to return your capital should the stock market fall, and if it rises you will receive most of the increase in your fund (but not necessarily all of it, so read the small print to find out what the guarantee covers).

The minimum investment period is usually five years (it can vary from one to ten) and if you withdraw your money before that term is up you will usually lose the guarantee and may have to pay early-surrender penalties. The guarantee comes at a price, so you may be better off investing your money for maximum growth rather than for safety.

Broker bonds

These are managed bond funds that are run by financial advisers who will 'manage' your investments by switching between life insurance funds to earn the highest rate of return. The minimum investment is usually £1000 and there may be a minimum investment term of five years.

How to find out more

Money Management magazine produces lists of bonds currently available.

Friendly Societies

These offer tax-exempt savings plans that are free of income and capital gains tax. However, you must tie up your savings for ten years and if you withdraw your money before then you will face high surrender penalties. The maximum investments are low – only £270 a year for single investments and £25 a month for regular savings. They should be considered as an addition to your investment porfolio if only because the investment limits are low and you should hardly miss the small monthly sum you invest. But the charges can be high.

Other Investment Options

Most other investment options require high lump-sum investments. Both Venture Capital Trusts and Enterprise Investment Schemes, which offer investments in newer companies, offer significant tax relief – 20 per cent at the time of investing and no capital gains tax on any profits – and have a minimum investment period of five years. A yield of 4 per cent increases to 30 per cent after tax relief. Minimum investments vary from £500 (single companies) to £2000 (a fund). However, the July 1997 Budget stopped companies from offering guarantees of a minimum return to investors, which makes these schemes increasingly risky.

Life assurance?

Here's a **low-cost** alternative

£49,301 *of life cover for just* 20p* *a day*

How can you help safeguard your family's financial future for less than the price of your daily newspaper? With the Legal & General Family Protection Plan. For just 20p* a day (£6.08 a month), a lump sum is paid should you die or become eligible for terminal illness benefit. For that premium, a non-smoking man aged 30 could get £49,301 of cover for 15 years. But the real advantage is you choose the term of the policy and the amount of cover you require or the monthly contribution that suits you. So if you'd prefer life assurance that isn't a lifetime commitment, call for a no-obligation quote today.

To receive a free Legal & General pen call free now, alternatively return the reply card at the back of this book.

Lines open 8AM – 8PM *weekdays,* 9AM – 5PM *weekends*

0500 33 66 66

Please quote reference number B26/GG01 when you call

Legal & General

*The equivalent of £6.08 a month. For your protection, calls will usually be reeorded and randomly monitored. Now and then, we may tell you about other products or services offered by the Legal & General Group of companies that we believe may be of interest to you. If you would prefer not to receive this carefully selected information, please contact us. Legal & General Direct Limited is a representative only of the Legal & General marketing group, members of which are regulated by the Personal Investment Authority and IMRO for the purposes of recommending, advising on and selling life assurance and investment products bearing Legal & General's name. Legal & General Direct Limited. Registered in England No. 2702080. Registered Office: Temple Court, 11 Queen Victoria Street, London EC4N 4TP.

7 Pensions

There's no time like the present.

Retirement may seem a long way off – after all it may be thirty or forty years away – but it is essential to start thinking about your pension as soon as possible, particularly in light of the July 1997 Budget which reduced the tax benefits of pension funds, and the recent Government proposals to introduce a new type of personal pension.

If you work for a medium to large sized company you have probably already been forced to think about your pension as you may have been asked to join your occupational pension scheme. Or you may have already started to invest in a personal pension plan. But if you have not made any pension provision then this should concentrate your mind:

▧ Could you live off £62.45 a week? That is the current value of the basic State pension.

▧ The State pension is permanently being eroded. It keeps pace with inflation, not with earnings. As a result it will have fallen from almost 25 per cent of national average earnings to less than 15 per cent by the year 2000. By the time you come to retire it will probably be worth only 8 per cent of average pay.

▧ If you do not invest in a pension you are wasting valuable tax relief. For every £600 a higher rate taxpayer invests in a pension, the tax man pays in £400. And there could be restrictions on tax relief in the future so make the most of it now.

▇ Your retirement can easily be half as long as your working life. So for every two years that you work you will have to invest enough in your pension to finance one year of retirement. A woman retiring at sixty can expect twenty years of retirement and a man more than sixteen.

The Cost of Delay

If you delay investing in a personal pension for just five years at the age of 25, when you come to retire your pension fund will be worth £127,000 or 35 per cent less (assuming a £100 per month investment that grows by 9 per cent a year).

A 25-year-old on average earnings will need to save roughly £150 a month out of taxed income in order to retire on a pension of two-thirds of final salary at 65. By the time he or she has risen up the career ladder and become a higher earner at the age of 35, the contributions will have to have risen to as much as £7200 a year (£360 a month plus £240 tax relief). These figures assume that you make regular contributions.

Remember, the earlier you start, the less you have to invest each month, and the longer you invest the more your pension fund investment will grow. Money doubles after eight years if the investment growth is 9 per cent. It increases five-fold within 19 years.

The Pension Options

SERPS

In addition to the basic state pension, you may qualify for an additional state pension, SERPS – the State Earnings Related Pension – which was introduced in 1975 for those not in occupational schemes (employer schemes are usually opted out of this). To qualify, you pay slightly higher National Insurance contributions. The self-employed are not eligible to join the scheme. The pension depends on your earnings in the years you have qualified for SERPS.

In 1986 legislation was introduced giving workers the right to opt out of the scheme and invest rebated National Insurance contributions in a personal pension. This is known as 'contracting out'. Members of an employer's scheme are automatically contracted out.

Contracting out of SERPS

If you contract out of SERPS the National Insurance rebates _must_ be paid into a personal pension plan. You can have a rebate-only personal pension plan, which means that you make no contributions of your own, but this is inadvisable as the contributions will be too small to adequately provide for your retirement. If you join a company scheme or are no longer employed you no longer qualify for SERPS rebates.

The rebate is based on your earnings between £3224 and £24,180 (for the 1997–98 tax year). Your rebates are a set percentage of earnings between these bands.

National insurance rebates for those contracting out of SERPS (Age at April 5 1997)

3.4 per cent at 16	4.5 per cent at 35
3.6 per cent at 20	5.4 per cent at 40
3.9 per cent at 25	8.2 per cent at 45
4.2 per cent at 30	9 per cent between 46 and 63

So if you earn £20,000 a year and are aged 25 your rebate will be as follows:

£20,000 – £3224 = £16,776 × 3.9% = £654.26

The pension you receive from your SERPS rebates depends on how well the personal pension fund performs and the charges.

£ CASH TIP £

Younger workers (under 45 for a man and 40 for a woman) earning at least £10,000 to £12,000 a year should opt out of Serps now if they have not done so already. This is partly because the future of SERPS is uncertain so it is worth taking the rebates and investing them in a personal pension while you still can.

£ CASH TIP £

If you have contracted out of SERPS you should increase your contributions to your personal pension. Until April 1997 rebates for those under 30 were 4.8 per cent. Now they are betwen 3.4 and 3.9 per cent. This cut means that you will have a shortfall.

£ CASH TIP £

Investing SERPS rebates in a personal pension can be expensive. Some insurance companies charge a fixed fee that can eat into smaller investments. A percentage charge can work out better than a set charge. If the fund is small – say £1000 – or you stop qualifying for SERPS, charges will still be taken out of your fund, reducing or negating any investment growth.

Contracting back into SERPS

If you have contracted out of SERPS, you can at a later date contract back in. Why? Because older workers gain more by being a member of SERPS than younger ones.

The cut-off age is over 45 to 49 for men and over 40 to 46 for women, depending on earnings and past contributions. So bear this in mind as you get older (if SERPS is still going then).

Occupational/Company Pension Schemes

Some ten million people belong to employers' pension schemes. These are usually the best way to plan for retirement because:

▮ your employer contributes to your pension, making this a valuable perk

▮ you usually receive additional benefits such as life insurance

▮ as with personal pensions you receive tax relief at your highest rate

In most cases, if you are given the opportunity to join an occupational scheme you should do so. Company pensions are only unwise for those expecting to stay a very short time with their employer (less than two years) and those who expect to job-hop on a frequent basis. The other advantage of company schemes is that they are enforced saving. Contributions to these are taken directly from your salary, saving you from making the decision of how much to pay and what pension provider to select.

The rules

▮ You cannot contribute to a company pension scheme and a personal pension (unless you have additional earnings other than from your employment to fund a personal pension plan).

▮ You can invest up to 15 per cent of your earnings in total.

On average, employees pay around 5 per cent of their salary into their employer's scheme and the employer adds a further 10 per cent. So if £300 a month is invested in your scheme you contribute £100. Your contributions automatically qualify for tax relief. So they only cost you £77 as a basic-rate taxpayer and £60 as a higher rate taxpayer. If you took out a personal pension plan you would have to make up at least some of your employer's contributions.

This is why occupational schemes are usually better investments than personal pensions. To make the same contributions to a personal pension you would have to invest £231 as a basic rate taxpayer and £180 as a higher rate taxpayer. Over your working life these additional contributions will mount up to a significant sum. Over 30 years as a basic rate tax payer you would have to pay £83,160 into a personal pension and only £27,720 into a company pension scheme to achieve the same investment.

Some employers offer a non-contributory scheme. This does not mean that your employer does not pay into the scheme – it is you, the employee, who does not have to make contributions.

Most employers' pension schemes offer additional benefits such as life insurance and a pension for dependants (often your children as well as your spouse) should you die while you are still in the scheme. If you want these extra benefits with a personal pension you will normally have to pay extra.

The costs of running the pension scheme are borne by the employer and as such there is less of an impact on your contributions. With personal pensions you must bear these charges yourself.

Employer pension schemes must now give equal rights to both men and women. As a result, many schemes now have increased the retirement age for women from 60 to 65.

The different types of occupational scheme

Final salary: Nine in ten employees who contribute to a company pension are in these schemes.

Final salary scheme pensions are based on:

- your salary at or near retirement (either final salary or average salary over the last three years before retirement)

- how long you have been a member of the scheme

You will receive a fraction of your salary – usually 1/60th of your final pay for each year you have been a member of the scheme. So after twenty years you will receive 20/60ths or one-third of your final pay. The maximum you can receive is two-thirds of your final salary (40/60ths). It is usually possible to boost your pension by 'buying' extra years of pension contributions.

PLANNING FOR PROSPERITY OR WALKING ON EGGS?

OLD MUTUAL winner of twelve Micropal Awards for fund performance in 1996.

You too can plan for your retirement with a company who provide consistent investment performance.

To find out more about Old Mutual and how we can help you phone 0345 585124.

OUR CLIENTS ARE PLANNING FOR PROSPERITY

Old Mutual Life Assurance Company Limited
Providence House, 2 Bartley Way, Hook, Hampshire, RG27 9XA.
Registered office: As above. Registered No. 943621 England.
Regulated by the Personal Investment Authority.

Please remember that past performance is not necessarily a guide to future investment performance. The price of units and income from them can go down as well as up as a result of changes in the value of underlying securities or currency movement. An investor may not get back the original amount invested.

The workplace and economic environment are ever changing. We need change to move forward and as a result our employment patterns have altered and many people are now working on a contract or freelance basis. This means that more of us have to make our own pension provision, rather than relying on the ever diminishing State pension.

For those who are in permanent employment, employers may make pension provision for them. However, it is not always an option, especially as many employer's are not keen to set up company schemes due to the increased administration burden imposed on them by recent legislation. Therefore, more and more employees are having to make their own pension provision.

Personal pension plans are portable, flexible and tax efficient, allowing tax relief on contributions at the contributor's highest marginal rate of income tax, investment in tax exempt funds and tax-free lump sum at retirement age (up to 25% of the fund). The combination of these three tax advantages makes this form of saving for retirement highly attractive to taxpayers.

The sooner you start making provision for your retirement the more you will benefit from the long term investment, but do not fall into the trap of just looking at charges when choosing a provider. Ensure that you look at the global picture such as consistent long term fund performance, enhanced allocation rates for large contributions, the range of funds available to suit your investment profile, the provision of waiver of contribution and the flexibility you need to suit your personal circumstances.

It's A Question Of Choice

Old Mutual group has over 150 years experience in financial services, manages assets of over 29 billion on behalf of its clients world-wide and is the 3rd largest life assurance company in the world*. Old Mutual was awarded twelve micropal awards in 1996 alone for fund performance, they offer enhanced allocation rates of up to 4% on regular contributions over £75 gross per month, waiver of contribution at no extra cost, a choice of 17 pension funds and flexibility to suit your needs.

Choosing a pension provider is a major long term investment decision. Ensure you have all the facts before taking that final step.
Ranked by net income. Source Fortune Magazine.

Unlike other types of pension, your final salary pension is not dependent on investment performance but is guaranteed to be a set proportion of your earnings.

Money purchase schemes: Money purchase scheme pensions are based on the amount of money you and your employer had paid in, not on years of service or your earnings, so you are not guaranteed a set level of pension. With many money purchase schemes the employer does not contribute as much as they would to a final salary scheme.

How much you receive on retirement is based on:

▮ the level of your contributions and those of your employer

▮ the investment performance of the pension fund

▮ annuity rates when you retire (an annuity must be purchased to provide you with a pension for life)

Money purchase schemes often include life insurance but many do not offer as many extra benefits as final salary schemes.

Younger employees who expect to remain only a few years with the scheme and job-hop on a frequent basis, may find that money purchase schemes offer a better deal on pension transfers and deferred pensions (where you leave your pension behind when you move jobs) than final salary schemes.

Hybrid schemes: A few employers offer a mixture of both money purchase and final salary schemes but these are rare.

Group personal pensions: Some employers – particularly newer and smaller companies – do not have a company pension scheme but instead set up a cluster of personal pensions. Although these are run on a group basis they are owned by the employee and are much more portable, so employees can take their own personal personal pension pot with them if they move jobs (usually without financial penalty).

These schemes are set up by an insurer on behalf of the employer. However, unlike occupational schemes, the charges are paid by the employee.

The amount received on retirement depends on how much has been invested, the costs and charges, how well the pension fund has performed and annuity rates.

The advantage of these schemes over personal pensions is that the employer normally contributes. Many employers are reluctant to contribute to a personal pension (however, new Government proposals are likely to encourage – if not force – employers to contribute in the future).

The changes to occupational schemes

Recent legislative and budget changes are set to have a major impact on the 200,000 occupational pension schemes.

The Pensions Act drafted after the Maxwell pension scandal has increased the costs of running occupational pensions by as much as 2 to 3 per cent of payroll costs.

As a result, an increasing number of employers are switching away from final salary to money purchase schemes. This is because they cost the employer less. But lower contributions mean smaller pensions so it is up to the employee to pay in more.

Most employers are not forcing staff to switch, instead they are closing final salary schemes to new employees and making them join new money purchase schemes.

The abolition of tax credits for pensions (until the Budget of July 1997 pension schemes could reclaim the 20 per cent tax deducted on dividends) has also pushed up costs and is expected to lead even more employers to abandon final salary schemes. The National Association of Pension Funds estimates that the tax changes will cut by 15 per cent the pension income of someone aged 35 who starts saving through a money purchase scheme now.

Starting a new job

When you start a new job you will have several pension choices. These depend on whether or not your employer has an occupational scheme and if you are eligible to join it. If you can join and do not have a personal pension, you should generally do so unless you expect to spend only a short time with your employer (two years or less).

If you already have a personal pension your options are:

1   To make your personal pension 'paid-up', which means you no longer make contributions and leave it to grow, and then join your employer's scheme (you can not have both types of pension). However, you will still have to pay charges on your personal pension and there may be penalties for stopping contributions. If you later leave your employer's scheme you can start up your personal pension again.

2   To transfer your personal pension into the employer's scheme. However, in many cases you may find that transfer penalties wipe out a large chunk of your pension fund. If you are joining a final salary scheme, the money will be used to buy extra years in service in your employer's scheme or to fund a fixed amount of pension when you retire. If it is a money purchase scheme, the transfer will be added to your pension fund.

3   To keep your personal pension and ask if your employer will contribute to it.

4   To keep your personal pension and not join the employer's scheme. This will only be an option if you know you will spend only a short time with your employer.

Two in ten new recruits do not bother to join their company's pension scheme. If you decide not to, make sure you make your own private pension provision. Remember, you will have to contribute more to make up for the lack of employer's contributions.

If you are in a final-salary scheme that gives you two-thirds of your salary at retirement and you wanted the same pension on retirement from a personal pension you would have to contribute about 20 per cent of your salary on average from aged 25 to 65. However, the chances of your staying with the same employer for your entire career are slim so few employees will qualify for this maximum two-thirds pension.

If you have left a job where you were a member of the company pension scheme, your options are listed below, in the section 'Leaving an Occupational Scheme'.

What you should ask when joining a scheme

Although joining an employer's scheme is generally a wise choice there are still aspects of the pension scheme that you need to examine. When you join a scheme (or if you are already a member) ask the pension fund manager for a booklet detailing the scheme's benefits.

▌ How much do you and your employer contribute?

▌ What is the retirement date?

▌ What level of life cover is provided? Death-in-service payments are usually four times salary.

▌ Can you transfer money to your employer's scheme from former pension schemes?

▌ How much of the pension can you take as a lump sum on retirement?

▌ If you are forced to retire early by your employer or take voluntary early retirement how will your pension be affected?

▌ If you have to retire due to ill health what pension will you receive?

▌ Is there provision for spouse's/dependant's pensions if you die in service or in retirement? What proportion of the pension will this be and for how long is it paid?

▌ How will the pension be increased after retirement (this should be at least inflation or 5 per cent, whichever is the lower)?

▌ How often do you get a statement of the pension benefits you have built up?

▌ And, if it is a money purchase scheme, what is the investment record of the fund?

When you join a company pension scheme you should be given a copy of the annual report, plus the scheme rules if you want them. After that you can ask for the audited annual report, which will tell you how the pension fund is invested.

Leaving an occupational scheme

If you leave employment you have several options:

1   Leave your company pension where it is.
      If it is a final salary scheme, your pension will grow by 5 per cent a year or inflation, whichever is the lower. This is known as a 'deferred pension', and at a time when pay rises are not always keeping up with inflation this may seem a good option. But remember that between the time of leaving your scheme and retiring inflation could creep up to more than 5 per cent. Also, if you invested in a personal pension with good performance, it should grow by more than 5 per cent a year (however it will have to perform well enough to make up for personal pension charges and the loss of some of your pension fund when you transfer).
      If it is in a money purchase scheme your contributions will continue to be invested and grow until you retire or transfer to another pension scheme. So your

pension will depend on the investment performance of the pension fund manager.

2   Transfer your pension into the scheme run by your new employer. You cannot take the money as a lump sum (unless you were in the scheme for less than two years) – it has to be paid into another pension scheme.

3   Transfer your company pension into a personal pension plan. This will be an option if you are not eligible to join another occupational pension scheme, you become self-employed or expect to remain in your future jobs for only a few years at a time. You must consider whether this will be a long-term arrangement. If you switch your fund to a personal pension and then after a few years join an occupational pension scheme and leave your personal pension paid up, you could be penalized twice – once on the transfer from the occupational scheme and again on leaving your personal pension 'paid up'.

Pension transfers

If you transfer from a final salary scheme you will lose some of the pension you have built up (the transfer value is based on a complex calculation). This can leave you worse off than 'deferring' the pension (leaving the pension where it is).

With money purchase schemes you can transfer the pension you have built up from your own and some of your employer's contributions, however you will have to pay an administration charge.

If you transfer within two years of joining a company pension scheme the employer only has to refund you your contributions (not any employer contributions) less any tax relief you have been given (although some will give you a transfer to another pension). You may only get a fraction of the amount you paid in because investment fees or an administration charge will also be deducted. If the scheme is contracted out of SERPS, a sum will be deducted to restore your SERPS entitlement.

It will probably take four to six weeks for your employer to send you a transfer statement and then three to four months for the pension assets to be transferred to a new scheme.

The decision on whether or not to transfer will depend on:

▪ how good your old scheme is

▪ what the transfer value is

▪ how many years you have been in the scheme

▪ how many years you have until retirement

Who to ask

Ask the pension scheme manager for advice. Often you will be put in touch with an actuary or other scheme adviser who can help evaluate your options. You should also visit an independent financial adviser. It is essential that you seek professional advice, as making the wrong decision could leave you thousands of pounds poorer when you come to retire.

Personal Pensions

If you are not a member of a company pension scheme the other major option to plan for your retirement is using a personal pension plan.

It is essential that you select your pension with great care, as picking a pension with high charges and poor performance could leave you with half the pension that you would have received had you invested in one of the top performing schemes. The Government is considering a new type of personal pension that will have lower charges and almost guaranteed performance as the fund will track the FTSE 100 Index. The proposals also include forcing employers to pay into employees' personal pensions. This will make them a more viable alternative to occupational schemes.

The rules

Those aged between 16 and 75 who have taxable earnings can invest in a personal pension that can be taken from age 50 (for post 1 July 1988 pensions) and taken even if you have not retired (something not allowed by occupational schemes). You can only invest a set percentage of your earnings and these qualify for tax relief at your highest rate.

You can also pay five per cent of your personal pension contributions into a life insurance policy that pays out on death before age 75. You can therefore get tax relief on life insurance contributions.

You cannot invest in a company/occupational pension scheme and a personal pension at the same time unless you have additional earnings from your main employment to cover your contributions to a personal pension.

When you retire you can take up to 25 per cent of the value of your pension fund as a tax-free lump sum. The remainder must be used to buy an annuity that will be invested to provide you with a pension once you retire. However, the rules on this have been relaxed. This is known as the 'open-market' option and it means you can draw an income from their pension rather than buying an annuity straight away and have up until age 75 to shop around for the best annuity deal.

Could you live off £62.45 a week?

Probably not, but that's current State pension for a single person and a reality facing many of today's pensioners who don't have their own pension. Will you be in that unhappy situation when you retire?

It doesn't look as if the State pension is likely to improve either. According to the Equal Opportunities Commission, the basic State pension in 1994 was 16% of national average earnings, but by 2030 it is forecast to be half that.

If you are among the millions not covered by a personal pension plan you need to seek advice fast. Even if you are in a company pension scheme it is estimated that only 1 in 100 people in a company pension scheme will retire on maximum benefits. *

Not only would a pension bring peace of mind but is it also the most tax efficient way of planning ahead as the Inland Revenue allows full tax relief on your pension contributions - 23% for a basic rate taxpayer and 40% for higher tax payers.

Bradford & Bingley is the largest financial institution on the high street to offer independent financial advice. Because they don't have their own pension and aren't tied to offering anybody else's they can help by giving impartial advice from amongst the best pension products on the market to find one that suits your demands and personal circumstances. The advice that they offer is completely free and without obligation.

* Source - Occupational Pensions. December 1992

How much you receive when you retire depends on:

▉ how much you pay in

▉ how long you pay contributions

▉ the charges

▉ any penalties for breaks in contributions

▉ the investment performance

▉ the annuity rates at the time you retire (annuities provide you with a pension for life)

The limits on contributions rise with age. The percentage limits only apply on earnings up to £84,000 (for 1997–98) and this earnings cap generally rises in line with inflation each year. (See Table 2.)

However, the chances are that you will not pay in anywhere near the maximum.

Table 2: Personal pension contribution limits

Age on 6 April 1997	% of pay	Maximum contribution
35 or under	17.5	£14,700
36–45	20	£16,800
46–50	25	£21,000
51–55	30	£25,200
56–60	35	£29,400
61 or over	40	£33,600

Are your regular savings growing fast enough in your building society?

Sort out a Flexible Savings Plan and your money could grow faster. It's easy.
Simply pick up the phone to the Blue Line and start saving from as little as £30
a month. Or as much as you can afford.

If an unforeseen financial problem comes up, no problem.
You can stop payments for a while. It's simple. No pressure. No jargon.
Get on the Blue Line now, direct to Friends Provident.
The people who know a thing or two about making money grow.

Call us on 0800 00 00 80

Get on the Blue Line

We're open 8 to 8 Weekdays. 10 to 4 Weekends.

FRIENDS PROVIDENT

The minimum that can generally be paid into a personal pension plan is £30 a month or £1000 as a one-off lump sum.

Should you be investing in a personal pension?

If you are not a member of an occupational scheme, in most cases you will be advised to take out a personal pension. However if your earnings are sporadic or you are on a short-term contract and do not know if you will still be earning in six month's time, you may be better off selecting a more flexible investment until your circumstances are more stable.

Pensions are a long-term investment and you can face hefty financial penalties if you continually stop and start your payments into your plan, however you should find that personal pensions are increasingly flexible. The alternative is to invest in a series of single premium personal pensions that do not require regular investment and tend to have lower charges.

How much should you pay in?

The answer to this has to be 'as much as possible'. Assuming a 6 per cent growth rate in performance, a man aged thirty earning £15,000 a year would have to pay in almost the maximum allowed to get a pension worth a third of his salary at retirement. To get half pay at retirement, contributions would exceed the limits allowed. However, much depends on investment performance. If returns average 12 per cent he would have to pay in less than £70 a month to get half his salary as a pension.

Accountants Price Waterhouse calculate that you would have to start saving 20 per cent of your earnings from the age of thirty to build up a pension equal to two-thirds of your final salary at 65. If you delay starting pension provision until forty, you would have to set aside 30 per cent (assuming 9 per cent investment growth, 6 per cent salary rises per annum, and annuity rates with 8 per cent investment returns bought with the pension fund on retirement).

If, as you climb the career ladder, your pay increases you can increase the amount you pay into your personal pension. If, on the other hand, you are finding your finances are stretched you can reduce your contributions. Always check the terms and conditions of your policy to find out how often you can change your contributions and if there are any financial penalties.

Tax relief

Tax relief at the basic rate is automatically invested in your personal pension. So to contribute £100 a month you will pay £77 and the Inland Revenue a tax rebate of £23. However, if you are a higher rate taxpayer you will have to claim the additional tax relief (£17) using your tax return. This tax relief means that every £100 a month invested in your personal pension only costs you £60.

However, if you pay higher rate tax on a small proportion of your earnings, tax relief will only be given on the amount of earnings taxed at the top rate. So if you pay 40 per cent tax on £1000 of earnings you will only get higher rate tax relief on £1000 of pension contributions.

To make the most of tax relief on pensions you can backdate or carry forward your contributions. If you have not used up the maximum tax relief for the last tax year you can backdate contributions. This will be particularly useful if you have paid in the maximum allowed in the current tax year or you were a higher rate taxpayer in the last tax year but are now a basic-rate taxpayer (you will therefore get tax relief at a higher rate instead of basic rate).

Different types of personal pension plans

There are three main types of fund:

- unit-linked
- with-profits
- unitized with-profits

In addition you can either pay a regular monthly premium or a series of lump sums.

Unit-linked: These are the most common type of personal pension. With unit-linked funds your money buys units of the investment fund and the value of these units can rise and fall depending on how well the fund and the stock market is performing.

When you invest in a unit-linked fund you may be given a choice of funds, however most investors in personal pensions opt for 'managed', which tend to be safer as the fund holdings are spread across a range of investments. UK funds are the second most popular and a few investors do opt for more specialist funds that can be more risky although they can also produce higher returns. Often you can split your investments and invest in two or three different funds, and can switch funds – often once a year without financial penalty – if your investment aims change or you are unhappy with the performance of the fund.

With-profits funds: This means that you share in the profits of a fund rather than buying a share or unit of that fund. The with-profits fund invests in a range of UK and overseas shares, bonds and cash. Each year you receive a bonus – known as the annual or reversionary bonus – which is your share of the profits of the fund. If the fund manager feels that investment returns are likely to be lower in future, bonuses may be reduced to reflect this. But once you have earned an annual bonus it cannot be taken away. With unit-linked funds if there is a stock market crash a chunk of your pension can be wiped out.

When you come to retire you earn a final or terminal bonus. The value of this can rise and fall depending on the investment performance of the fund. The level of final bonus is not guaranteed so you should pick a plan that does not rely too heavily on this final payment.

Unitized with-profits plans: These are newer types of plans and are a combination of unit-linked and with-profits schemes. As with unit-linked funds you buy units in the fund but these units increase when annual bonuses are added, in a similar way to with-profits plans. Once bonuses have been added they cannot be taken away. This makes these schemes less risky than unit-linked plans.

Unit/investment trust plans: These tend to have lower charges as they invest in unit trusts and investment trusts with their lower charging structures. However, they are more risky than unitized with-profits and conventional with-profits plans.

Regular and/or single premiums: Most employees earning a regular income will prefer to pay monthly contributions to their personal pension. However, if these regular payments are not maintained there can be penalties to pay. If you are self-employed or have an irregular income, a single premium pension plan may be a better alternative. These schemes allow you to pay a single or a series of lump sums.

The charges on single premium pension plans tend to be far lower than for regular premium plans. Initial charges can be as low as 1 per cent and annual management fees around 0.5 per cent, although in some cases charging structures can be more complicated and more expensive. Check that you can make extra ad hoc payments – for instance if you receive a large annual bonus – at any time.

However, investing on a one-off basis does have its risks. The advantage of regular investing is that this irons out the fluctuations in the stock market. With a single premium investment you have to be more aware of the timing of your investments.

Choosing a personal pension

The main aspects to evaluate are:

- performance

- charges

- portability and flexibility – these are important particularly if you plan to take a career break, or worry that you may have periods of unemployment or may decide to join an occupational scheme at a later date

Comparing performance

When you are given an illustration of the value of your pension on retirement, the financial adviser will quote you a standard investment performance rate. These projections were standardized to stop salesmen quoting unrealistic levels or return. So all companies must give you a quote of your retirement fund assuming 6, 9 and 12 per cent growth.

Although it is impossible to predict how well your pension fund investments will perform, you can get a good idea of the quality of the fund management by comparing past performance. Companies that are consistently among the top performers, reflecting good fund management and low-charging structures, are listed in magazines like *Money*

Management, which are available in libraries and newsagents. However, remember that past performance is no guarantee of future performance.

Over 15 years with-profits funds have produced higher returns than unit-linked managed funds, although the difference in performance has narrowed. But over twenty to thirty years unit-linked plans tend to perform better. But unit-linked plans can be more volatile, and the worst performing with-profits fund over the last 15 years has produced more than double the returns of the worst performing unit-linked pension.

The costs of picking a poor-performing fund

Over the last twenty years £200 a month in the best performing personal pension would now be worth £360,025 after total premiums of £48,000. However, the worst performing fund would be worth just £200,000 – £160,000 less. If someone stole £160,000 from you, imagine how you would feel.

Warning: You will have to invest more in your personal pension fund following the July 1997 Budget. Pension funds can no longer reclaim the 20 per cent tax credit on dividends. This means that instead of receiving the full dividend, pension funds will now only get 80p in every £1. It will reduce the yield of the average pension fund investing in UK shares from 4 per cent to 3.2 per cent.

Charges

Charges can reduce your final pension by a third. These charges cover the cost of administering your personal pension, paying commission to financial advisers and sales people, marketing and advertising, and fund management. If you are a basic-rate taxpayer then these costs can, in some cases, wipe out the benefits of tax relief. Salesmen can be paid up to £2500 for selling a personal pension and sometimes as little as 89 per cent of your contributions are invested in the first five years.

An employee saving £100 a month in a personal pension over 35 years would be £65,000 worse off with a high-charging plan than one with low charges (assuming 9 per cent growth) according to a survey by *Which? Magazine*. Think how hard you would have to work to earn that much after tax – as a higher rate taxpayer more than £100,000. The same survey found that the lowest charging plan reduced your overall pension by 13 per cent and the highest charging plan by 35 per cent.

Financial advisers are required to give you details of costs. However, they only have to show you how charges will affect the pension they are recommending (this will be detailed in the Key Features Document), so ask how charges compare with other personal pensions.

Charges are disclosed in several ways:

- by showing you how charges will reduce investment performance, assuming a set rate of investment growth

- by showing you how much you would be given as a surrender value in the first five years and then in years 10, 15, 20 and 25 should you want to transfer your personal pension

- by giving you an indication of how much the total charges could amount to over the full term of the policy

Portability and flexibility

The days when you joined a firm from school or college and remained with that company until retirement are long gone. So, as with all your financial plans, you must plan your pension with this in mind. Some pensions are more flexible than others and allow you to take contribution breaks (for instance during maternity leave or if you are made redundant or join an occupational scheme). Always check the financial penalties imposed.

Some plans allow you to suspend contributions and pay reduced fees during these periods, while others may impose high charges.

If you are likely to change jobs and move to a company with an occupational scheme you should also check that the personal pension plan does not charge heavily for transferring your pension fund. The other advantage of picking a personal pension that is easily portable is that if you are unhappy with the investment performance you can switch your pension to another investment company.

Transfer values can vary dramatically. If you had been paying £50 a month into your plan for two years and had paid in total premiums of £1200, some providers would give you £1310 as a transfer value (assuming 9 per cent investment growth). However, with others you would get back just half the amount you had invested.

Most of the charges with unit-linked pensions are usually taken out of your contributions in the first few years, so your transfer value may be lower than the amount you have paid into the plan. With-profits schemes tend to spread the charges over the whole term of the policy.

Waiver of premiums – a must

Check your personal pension has a 'waiver of premium' option. This covers your pension contributions if you are unable to work as a result of illness or accident. Fewer than one in three of those with personal pensions have taken out this insurance and as a result risk losing out on their pension should they no longer be able to earn an income. The costs usually add between 1.5 and 5 per cent to the cost of the monthly premium.

However, the policy terms and conditions vary. In some cases the policy does not pay out for six months, and some specify that you must be unable to do any job at all, but with others you can claim if you cannot follow your own occupation.

Getting the right advice

You have probably read about the personal pension mis-selling scandal. Between 1988 and 1994 some 570,000 members of occupational schemes and SERPS were wrongly advised to take out personal pensions. They may have lost as much as £4 billion. The pensions industry has already been warned to speed up the investigation of these cases as already 20,000 policy holders have died and fewer than 18,000 have received any compensation.

Do not let this scandal put you off investing for retirement. Even a poor pension will be better than no pension at all when you come to retire.

The regulatory spotlight on the selling of personal pensions should mean that you will receive sound advice, and you should find that you are not automatically recommended a personal pension (which earns the salesman commission) instead of being advised to join or stay with your employer's pension scheme (which earns an adviser no commission at all). By paying a fee-based financial adviser you will have any commission the adviser would have earned paid into your personal pension plan.

Some personal pension providers do not pay commission to financial advisers, so if you are using an independent financial adviser ask if the recommendations include personal pensions from these providers as well as those that pay commission.

Watch out for direct or telephone selling organizations that offer 'execution only' personal pensions and do not give advice. The problem is that if you buy the wrong personal pension you forfeit your right to protection against bad advice under the Financial Services Act. As you have made the investment decision, if it turns out to be the wrong one the only person you can blame is yourself.

If possible, go to an adviser who specializes in pensions. The Society of Pension Consultants can supply you with a list of independent pensions advisers in your area (telephone 0171 353 1688).

Monitoring your personal pension

Contributing to a personal pension is the first step. Contributing enough to fund a comfortable retirement is the next. Although you may not be able to afford a high level of contributions today, you should ask on a regular basis how much you should be investing and aim to meet these contribution requirements in the future. That is why you should make sure you have a long-term relationship with your financial adviser.

You should also monitor the investment performance of your personal pension. If your pension performs badly you can consider switching your pension to another investment company. However, as discussed above, you will be penalized for doing so. Even so, it may pay to switch your fund as although you could lose a few thousand pounds now, over the thirty or so years to retirement you could more than recoup these losses and gain far more. Always seek advice before deciding to switch pensions.

Alternatively you can stop contributing to your existing personal pension – known as making your plan 'paid-up' – and take out another personal pension with a better performing company. You will have to pay two lots of charges, but these will probably not add up to as much as you would pay if you transferred your personal pension into another scheme.

Finally, you can keep paying into your existing pension to avoid any charges and take out a second personal pension with a better preforming investment company.

The new stakeholder pension

At the time of writing this is still a Government proposal. It will be a personal pension in addition to SERPS and the current personal pensions, and will be aimed at those who are not members of occupational schemes and who have not taken out a personal pension. One option is to give investors in these schemes a National Insurance rebate similar to that given to those who opt out of SERPS. The new pension is likely to be compulsory for those who have no private pension provision.

£ CASH TIP £

The new Stakeholder pensions will be low cost, flexible and secure. However, you can already get these features with personal pensions provided you shop around. The security will come from the fact that Stakeholder pensions will invest in 'tracker funds' – low-charging investment funds that track the performance of the stock market (many fund managers fail to match this performance). These tracker funds are already available. Personal pensions are also increasingly flexible and some have lower charges than others, so it is up to you to shop around.

Self-invest pensions

Known as Sipps (self-invested personal pensions), these are aimed at high earners who want to manage the investment of their pension. The advantages are that you can choose a range of investments, including UK and foreign stocks as well as commercial property, life funds and unit trusts. The tax reliefs are the same as for ordinary personal pensions. However, the charges tend to be higher so they will only appeal to those contributing at least £10,000 a year to their pension fund.

Alternatives to personal pensions

If you are freelance, self-employed, or know that your career means that you will have periods when you do not earn a regular wage, you can consider alternative investments that have lower charges. However, remember that you will not qualify for tax relief, which is the major advantage of pensions. Currently, the favoured alternative is a the tax-free Personal Equity Plan. However this is to be replaced by the new Individual Savings Account in 1999. The advantages of other stock market based investments are that charges can be lower, you have greater flexibility on contributions, there are no contributions limits, you can take your lump sum at any time (so you could retire at 45 if you invest enough), and you do not have to buy an annuity. With personal pension plans at least 75 per cent of your retirement fund must be used to buy an annuity to provide you with an income for life.

Is this the *ideal* pension?

Looking for a personal pension plan that offers *all* the essential benefits and assurances? You're looking at it now.

- ○ *Index-tracking for growth potential* ✓
- ○ *Fully portable from job to job* ✓
- ○ *Freedom to vary payments* ✓
- ○ *Stop and start payments to suit your circumstances** ✓
- ○ *Payment protection option†* ✓

And you can start your pension plan from just £50 a month. Call us without obligation on 0500 65 65 65.

Legal & General

Take the FIRST STEPS to starting your PENSION now

0500 65 65 65

Lines open 8AM – 8PM weekdays, 9AM – 5PM weekends
Call now, quoting reference B10/GY01 or talk to your financial adviser.
For your protection, calls will usually be recorded and randomly monitored.

Call free now. Or to receive a free Legal & General pen please return the reply card at the back.

*Subject to Legal & General's approval. This will affect the value of your pension. †Waiver of contribution. The value of units may go down as well as up. Now and then we may tell you about our other products or services offered by the Legal & General Group of companies that we believe may be of interest to you. If you would prefer not to receive this carefully selected information, please contact us. Legal & General Direct Limited is a representative only of the Legal & General marketing group, members of which are regulated by the Personal Investment Authority and IMRO for the purposes of recommending, advising on and selling life assurance and investment products bearing Legal & General's name. Terms and conditions available on request. Legal & General Direct Limited. Registered in England No. 2702080. Registered Office: Temple Court, 11 Queen Victoria Street, London EC4N 4TP.

8 Mortgages

Rent money is dead money.

Your home is likely to be one of the biggest investments you ever make. But while it may take you months or even years to find your ideal home, the chances are you will put comparatively little thought into choosing the right mortgage for your needs. It is only when you compare the different interest costs over the lifetime of the mortgage that you realize just how much you can save by shopping around for the best mortgage deal.

Homebuyers could save almost £8000 over the life of a 25-year £50,000 interest-only mortgage by going to the best-value lender instead of the worst, according to *What Mortgage* magazine. Local building societies performed well in the survey, and generally building societies were cheaper than banks.

However, with as many as 4000 different mortgage products on offer at any one time, it can be very difficult to decide which will offer you the best value.

Consumer protection

Mortgages and now covered by the Code of Mortgage Lending Practice. Under this code of practice lenders can provide three levels of service:

▨ proper advice, which means you should be recommended the best mortgage for you

▨ full information, which means you will only be given details about a particular lender's mortgages

▨ information on one mortgage, which means you will only be given details about the home loan you are interested in

Lenders must make it clear which level of service they are providing.

How Much Can I Borrow?

This is the first thing you need to know so that you can start looking for properties in your price bracket. Generally you will be required to put down a deposit of at least 5 per cent of the purchase price, although it is possible to take out a 100 per cent home loan that requires no deposit at all.

To get the best deals, you will generally need a much larger deposit of up to 25 per cent of the purchase price.

Generally, you can borrow three times your annual salary if you are buying alone. If you are buying with a partner you can borrow up to 2.5 times joint salaries, or three times the main salary plus the additional salary.

If part of your earnings is made up of commission or bonuses you may be able to add these to your salary to boost the amount you can borrow. However, your lender will want to see proof that these payments are reasonably consistent and will probably require your employer to put this in writing.

If you are self-employed you will generally have to supply three year's of audited accounts. So if you are thinking of becoming self-employed at a later date, take a mortgage out while you are still an employee.

Non-status Mortgages

Anyone without a regular income can opt for a non-status mortgage. This does not require proof of income. Generally the loan must not be more than 75 per cent of the property's value. However, these loans come at a price, with interest rates often 2 or 3 per cent above the standard variable rate.

Mortgage Brokers

These often help those who may otherwise find it hard to get a mortgage. Fees for their services are usually 1 per cent of the loan.

Guarantors

The alternative way to boost the amount you can borrow is to ask someone – usually your parents – to act as a guarantor. If you cannot meet the payments they will then become liable.

£ CASH TIP £

In the current fast-moving property market (some homes are selling within days) it is advisable to arrange your mortgage in advance of looking for properties. Often estate agents will want to know you have the finance before showing you properties. And if you have a mortgage pre-arranged you will reduce the risks of being gazumped (when you lose the property because another buyer offers a higher price in the time it takes for you to complete your purchase).

> **Warning:** Remember that interest rates can rise. In the late 1980s mortgage rates topped 15 per cent and millions of home buyers struggled to meet their repayments. Check you will still be able to afford your mortgage if interest rates rose to double figures once again.

Choosing a Mortgage

There are several things you must consider.

Different Types of Mortgage

Repayment mortgage

Each month you pay interest on the amount outstanding and repay an element of your outstanding debt.

Pros:

▪ Safe – if you make all the payments your loan will be repaid at the end of the mortgage term.

▪ You do not have to rely on an endowment or other repayment vehicle to perform well enough to repay the outstanding loan.

▪ If you switch mortgages you do not have to worry about cashing in your endowment or taking out an extra endowment policy to cover a larger mortgage.

▪ They are much easier to understand and select. With interest-only mortgages you have to compare interest costs and select the best performing repayment vehicle. With repayments you need only pick the best rate.

Cons:

▨ At the end of the mortgage you have no lump sum. With most endowment mortgages you can expect to repay the loan and receive an extra cash payment.

Do not forget to add in the costs of separate life assurance (term assurance) that must be taken out to pay off your loan if you die.

Interest-only mortgages

With these the homebuyer pays interest only on the outstanding loan and then contributes to an investment that should produce sufficient returns to pay off the loan at the end of the mortgage term. None of the outstanding debt is repaid until the end of the term or when you sell your property. The most popular interest-only mortgages are backed by endowments but they can also be linked to personal pensions and personal equity plans.

Pros:

▨ If your investment performs well you may have more than enough to repay your outstanding mortgage and have an extra tax-free lump sum on top.

▨ With good investment performance (and a flexible repayment investment) you could be able to repay your loan early.

▨ Endowments (and usually pension plans) have life insurance built-in so you do not have to pay for extra life cover.

Cons:

▪ You do not repay any of the outstanding debt, so if you want to sell your property you will still have to repay the same size mortgage that you borrowed at the outset.

▪ The value of your investment/endowment may not be sufficient to repay your mortgage at the end of the term. If investment performance is poor you may have to increase your premiums to cover any potential shortfall.

Endowment mortgages

If you decide that you want an endowment mortgage, you must then select the type of endowment policy that will best suit your needs. In some cases you will not be given a choice and will have to take out the endowment policy that the lender sells (most are tied to or own life insurance companies).

In recent years there have been warnings that some endowments will not produce enough investment returns to meet the outstanding loan at the end of the mortgage. However, this problem has mainly been concentrated among those with short-term mortgages.

In most cases endowments need a growth of 8 to 10 per cent a year to pay off the debt. However even at the moment most ten-year policies are giving returns of around 10 per cent and 25-year plans around 13 per cent. However, performance does vary. So, in addition to picking a mortgage with a competitive mortgage rate, you must also pick one with a good performing endowment policy.

> **Warning:** If you need to cash in your endowment policy early or get into financial difficulties and can no longer afford the premiums you could get only a fraction of your investment returned. Once you have taken out an endowment policy you must keep paying the premiums for the full 25 years to get the maximum returns, and if you want to move up the property ladder you will have to take out additional endowment policies to cover the extra loan.

Different types of endowment policies

With-profits: With these you share in the profits of the life fund, with bonuses added annually. Once added to your fund these bonuses cannot be taken away, even if the stock market crashes. At the end of the policy term you receive a terminal or final bonus.

Unit-linked: With these your premiums buy units in a life fund and the value of these can rise or fall depending on the underlying performance of the fund. As a result, the value of your fund can drop if the stock market falls. In the last few years of the policy your investments are switched to safer funds to prevent a stock market crash wiping out some of your final pay-out. You may be given a choice of funds but will generally be advised to invest in a safe managed-fund.

Unitized with-profits: These are slightly newer types of endowment policy and combine features of both the others. You buy units in a fund but receive annual bonuses.

Performance of endowment policies

As discussed above it is essential to pick a good-performing endowment policy as well as a low mortgage rate, and in some cases a top performing endowment can earn you far more than any extra interest you have to pay on your home loan.

A man who took out a with-profits endowment 25 years ago (when he was aged 29) and paid in £50 a month would have received £96,767 on average from his endowment policy at the end of the term. But according to a survey by _Money Management_ magazine the difference between the top performing fund (which paid out £114,628) and the poorest performer (which paid out £65,611) was almost £50,000. If you took out a £60,000 mortgage that cost you an average of 8 per cent interest but could have taken out a cheaper mortgage that cost an average of 7.5 per cent, you would pay some £7000 in extra interest over the term of the mortgage. This extra interest would cost you nowhere near as much as the losses you could suffer by picking a poor-performing endowment policy.

PEP mortgages

These use a Personal Equity Plan as the investment vehicle to repay your mortgage. The advantages are that they are tax-free investments and much more flexible than endowments, so that if the fund performs well you can decrease or stop your payments or repay your mortgage early. The drawback of PEPs is that they are directly linked to the stock market and as such their value can rise as well as fall. Life insurance must be arranged separately.

Although PEP mortgages are still on offer, the Budget of 1997 announced that they would be replaced by a new savings scheme, the Individual Savings Account, in 1999. So they may not be available for much longer.

Pension mortgages

Remember that your pension is primarily there to provide an income for retirement. Although there are currently tax breaks on pensions, which means that you receive tax relief at your highest rate on contributions and a tax-free lump sum on retirement, these tax breaks may not be guaranteed by future governments. You usually need to arrange separate life insurance, although you can receive tax relief on some life insurance contributions if they are part of your personal pension.

Pros:

▊ Significant tax advantages.

Cons:

▊ You may have less money on which to retire and you will have used up this valuable tax break on a mortgage rather than your pension.

Flexible mortgages

These are relatively new types of home loan. You do not have to pay a fixed amount each month for the life of the mortgage, and can increase, decrease, or temporarily stop payments to suit your circumstances. These loans appeal to the self-employed, those with variable earnings, and those who expect to earn large bonuses that they want to use to pay off chunks of their mortgage.

Some flexible mortgages are linked to current accounts and work as a combined loan and current account. Flexible mortgages can also offer repayment breaks of up to six months. However, the rates may not be the lowest on the market.

Variable, Fixed, Capped or Discount?

Discounted and fixed rate mortgages now account for some 75 per cent of new home loans. However, because lenders can only give you the initial APR (the annual percentage rate of interest which reflects the true cost of borrowing) these can be difficult to compare. Always look at the cost of borrowing over the full term of the mortgage. And watch out for redemption penalties if you switch or cash in your mortgage, as in some cases you will have to pay a financial penalty of six months' interest.

Variable rate mortgages

The rate of most standard mortgages varies in line with interest rate moves. So you gain if rates fall but must bear the brunt of any interest rate rises. (See the section 'Annually Adjusted Mortgages' below.)

Pros:

▌ More flexible as you can usually cash in your mortgage without financial penalties.

Cons:

▌ If rates rise significantly you could find it difficult to meet your monthly mortgage payments.

Warning: Some lenders take longer than others to pass on interest rate reductions and some increase rates more quickly when they rise. Over the term of a mortgage the timing of rate moves can add considerably to the cost of your mortgage.

Annually adjusted mortgages

Some 40 per cent of variable rate mortgages have the monthly repayments adjusted annually – not when interest rates change. Although the amount of interest you are charged will change when interest rates rise and fall, your actual repayments do not. At the end of the year (usually in the spring) your monthly repayments will be adjusted to reflect any under or overpayment of interest. When interest rates rise you may find that you are paying far less for your home loan than those with standard variable mortgages. However, when rates fall you are likely to pay more. Over the lifetime of your mortgage you should not pay any more or less than with another type of home loan.

Pros:

▌ You know at the beginning of the year how much your monthly repayments will be.

Cons:

▌ If interest rates have risen significantly you could face a large increase in your monthly repayments once the annual adjustment takes place.

Fixed rate mortgages

Fixed rate mortgages are usually a safe option when interest rates are set to rise. However, you will find that rates are higher than variable mortgages if lenders believe rate rises are likely.

For instance, in the spring of 1997 some standard rate mortgages were cheaper than the fixed rates on offer. But as interest rates started to rise, those with fixed rates started to gain. So although you may be paying more initially you will win over the longer-run if interest rates rise as predicted.

The fixed rate usually applies for the first one to five years.

Pros:

▊ You know how much you will have to pay for the term of the fixed rate and if rates rise during the fixed period you will pay less than those with variable mortgages.

Cons:

▊ If rates are lower over the term of your fixed rate, you will pay more interest than with a variable loan.

▊ When the fixed rate ends you can find that your monthly mortgage payments jump significantly.

▊ These loans are less flexible and if you cash in your mortgage in the first few years you could have to pay several months' interest as a penalty.

Warning: Once the fixed rate period has finished you may be obliged to remain with the lender for a number of years or pay a financial penalty. So if the lender charges a higher than average rate you could lose out.

£ CASH TIP £

Do not take out a fixed rate mortgage if you expect that interest rates will fall to below the level of the fix during the fixed rate period.

£ CASH TIP £

Check that the loan is portable so that you can take it with you if you are moving up the property ladder. If it is not, and you need to cash in your mortgage, you will usually face financial penalties.

Warning: If you fall into arrears with a fixed rate loan the penalties can be much higher than with other mortgages. So ask before taking out the mortgage.

Capped rate mortgages

These are less common but will appeal at a time of rising mortgage rates as they guarantee that rates will not rise above a set level or cap. In some cases they are 'collared' which means that a minimum rate of interest has also been set so any rate reductions below this level will not apply. These are known as cap and collar mortgages. The capped rate can apply for anything from the first five years to the full term of the mortgage.

Pros:

▊ You know that for the period of the capped rate you will never pay more than a certain level of interest.

Cons:

▊ If you cash in your mortgage in the first few years you may have to pay financial penalties.

▨ If the mortgage also has a minimum interest rate you could find that if interest rates fall you will not get the benefit of very low mortgage rates.

Discount mortgages

These give you a discount of anything from 0.25 to 5 per cent off the variable rate of interest for the first few months or years of the mortgage.

These are only usually offered to:

▨ first-time buyers

▨ new borrowers (who have a mortgage from another lender)

▨ in some cases, existing borrowers coming back for a new loan

Pros:

▨ For the term of the discount you will pay less than other borrowers.

Cons:

▨ Check what rate will apply after the discount period has ended as you may have to pay a higher rate than other borrowers.

▨ There are usually high penalties for all or part repayment of the loan in the first few years, and borrowers may be required to repay all of the discount.

£ CASH TIP £

Check that the interest is discounted and not deferred. If it is deferred it will be added to the outstanding loan and you could end up with a larger mortgage than you started with.

Incentives

Tough competition between mortgage lenders means that most now offer first-time and new borrowers cash inducements.

Cashbacks

Some lenders refund a set percentage of the loan on completion, often refunding up to 5 per cent of the mortgage up to a maximum of £10,000 cashback, although the upturn in the housing market means these are now less common. However, there is often a price. You may have to pay up to 0.75 per cent above the standard variable mortgage rate (which can cost more in the long run than than the cashback) and you will also be tied into the mortgage for five or six years. If you redeem your mortgage before then you may have to repay the 'cashback'. The loans often have arrangement fees.

Free services

Some lenders offer to waive the valuation fee or pay for some of your legal costs.

Extra charges

The extra costs of taking out a mortgage are often overlooked. The actual cost of taking out a home loan can vary widely, even though on the surface there seems to be no difference in mortgage rates or terms.

Mortgage indemnity

This is an extra cost that many home buyers forget to budget for. It is an insurance charge that is paid by the borrower to protect against losses should the buyer fall into arrears. Although you as the buyer must pay the premium it protects the lender, not you. And if you are repossessed and the home is sold for less than the outstanding debt you could be pursued for the losses.

It must generally be paid by those taking out a home loan for more than 75 per cent of the property value. Mortgage indemnity is charged on a sliding scale and can rise to 10 per cent of the outstanding loan on a 100 per cent mortgage. But it is only paid on the proportion above 75 per cent. So on a £100,000 mortgage this will be 10 per cent of £25,000 or £2500. For 85 per cent mortgages the rate falls to about 6 per cent. But rates charged do vary. On a £60,000 mortgage you can pay between £555 and £1224 in mortgage indemnity insurance if you only have a 5 per cent deposit.

To help borrowers meet the costs lenders often allow the premium to be added to the mortgage loan. The snag with this is that the borrower will end up paying for it for 25 years. So if you can find an alternative way to finance it do your sums and you may find that over the longer run it is cheaper to pay for it using an alternative way of borrowing. Some lenders allow homebuyers to pay in 36 monthly instalments at the start of the loan.

£ CASH TIP £

A few lenders, including the Cheltenham and Gloucester no longer charge mortgage indemnity insurance. But this should not influence your mortgage choice entirely – weigh up the overall costs.

£ CASH TIP £

You cannot shop around for the best mortgage indemnity deal, as you must purchase the one arranged by your lender. But you can compare different lenders, as premiums do vary.

£ CASH TIP £

The larger the deposit the cheaper the mortgage indemnity. If possible, try to put down a deposit of 25 per cent to escape the premiums altogether. Find out what rates are charged on different sizes of loan. By putting down a slightly larger deposit (say, 6 per cent instead of 4 per cent) you may be able to save hundreds of pounds on your mortgage indemnity premiums.

Warning: Not all lenders call their extra charge Mortgage Indemnity Insurance. Some call it a High Lending Fee and others a Scheme for Maximum Advances. So you may not realize what you are paying for or the fact that it provides you with no protection at all.

Arrangement fees

In some case you may be charged an arrangement fee. Always ask in advance what this will be and if it will be refunded should you be forced to pull out of a property purchase.

Tied products

In some cases you may be required to take out buildings and contents insurance arranged by the lender as a condition of the loan. If the insurance is much more expensive than you can arrange elsewhere, you will lose out.

How Interest is Charged

Mortgages have been covered by 'annual percentage rate' rules since 1987. The APR should give the true cost of borrowing and include the cost of any arrangement fees, legal and valuations costs, and state the way interest is calculated. However, because the APR can be given on the initial fixed or discount rate it makes the true cost over 25 years very difficult to compare.

The best way to compare is the cost of nine monthly repayments over 25 years. Take into account any discounts or short-term fixed rates.

Also, you will find that interest is charged in different ways. Most building societies take payments in advance but bank mortgages are usually paid in arrears.

Repayment mortgages

Homebuyers could be paying £73 billion in unnecessary interest charges on their mortgage over the next 25 years because not all lenders calculate interest in the same way, according to calculations from Yorkshire Bank.

Most lenders calculate interest annually, basing the next 12 months' payments on the mortgage balance outstanding on the first day of the year. No account is made of payments credited to the repayment mortgage over the subsequent 12-month period. This costs borrowers some £160 million a year.

The other way that homebuyers lose is that only a few lenders calculate interest daily, working out interest on the balance outstanding at the end of each day. The total interest on a £51,000 repayment mortgage over 25 years, assuming an interest rate of 7.24 per cent, would be £60,783 if calculated on an annual basis. On a daily basis the total interest would be only £47,103.

Redemption Penalties

If you agree to pay redemption penalties (a charge if you cash in your mortgage within the first few years) you will usually be offered a lower mortgage rate. However, if you do need to move you could find that the savings of a fixed rate or discount mortgage do not make up for the redemption costs.

Warning: Think twice before making additional mortgage payments as some loans do not allow even part repayments of the mortgage without triggering redemption penalties.

£ CASH TIP £

In some cases lenders allow you to take your mortgage with you when you move. This way you avoid hefty redemption penalties – often totalling up to several thousand pounds.

Mortgage protection

Some 2.5 million of the 10 million homebuyers risk serious arrears on their mortgage payments if they become sick or unemployed. Cuts in social security mean that it is now advisable to buy insurance that will cover your monthly repayments. New borrowers receive no assistance with mortgage interest payments for the first nine months after stopping work.

It is usually easier and cheaper to take out this cover at the same time as your mortgage. You do not have to buy it from your mortgage lender and can shop around for a cheaper rate.

Lenders are now offering more than just mortgage protection insurance. Some offer a mix of life insurance, critical illness cover, permanent health insurance and unemployment cover in one policy.

Watch out for the small print. Some policies do not pay out until a policyholder has been off work for six months due to illness. And in the case of redundancy, payments often only start sixty days after employment ceases and then payments only last for a year or two.

Warning: Read the small print of your mortgage protection policy as you may find that you are excluded from cover as you are self-employed or you invalidate your policy if you move jobs.

Mortgage Term

Although most mortgages are taken over a 25-year period or term there is nothing to stop you choosing a shorter or longer payback term from ten to thirty years.

With a repayment mortgage, the shorter the term the higher the monthly costs. (See Table 3.)

With an interest-only loan, the length of the mortgage term makes no difference to the interest payments since the debt stays the same. However, you will have to invest more in either your endowment, PEP or pension plan to ensure that your investment is adequately funded to repay the loan at the end of the term. So if you want a shorter term mortgage, a repayment mortgage may be the better option.

If you cut a £100,000 mortgage term from 25 years to 15 years and pay an interest rate of 7.75 per cent you will pay £72,500 less interest over the term of the mortgage for an extra monthly repayment of less than £200. The only problem is that if you are borrowing near the maximum allowed and rates increase, you will probably find it hard to meet your monthly mortgage bill. However, you will be repaying the capital much faster so if you have to move you will have greater equity in the property. (See Table 3.)

Table 3: How reducing the mortgage term increases monthly repayments

Term of loan	Size of loan	
	£55,000	£75,000
	Monthly cost	
10 years	£653.05	£901.43
15 years	£505.47	£700.18
20 years	£436.82	£606.58
25 years	£399.36	£555.49

Source: Halifax – monthly payments assume 8 per cent interest and tax relief at 15 per cent on the first £30,000 (MIRAS will reduce to 10 per cent from April 1998). These are for repayment mortgages only.

Type of Lender

You no longer have the choice of just a bank or building society. Insurance companies, centralized lenders, and even telephone-based mortgage companies all offer home loans. Surveys have shown that the smaller, local building societies tend to offer cheaper mortgages over the longer term, but they do restrict who they will lend to. Whoever you decide to take a mortgage with, compare their long-term mortgage record to ensure that their rates are consistently competitive and that they pass on rate reductions quickly but are not the first to up their mortgage rates when interest rates rise.

MIRAS

Mortgage interest tax relief (MIRAS) is given on the first £30,000 of your loan. The current rate of tax relief is 15 per cent. However, this will be cut to 10 per cent from April 1998. (See Table 4.)

The Costs of Buying a Home

On a flat or house costing just over £30,000 you will have to find around £1000 to cover the mortgage setup and purchase costs. These costs rise to £4000 on a £100,000 property with a 95 per cent mortgage, and these purchase costs do not include the deposit and extras such as furnishings and fittings, which will push the total bill to well over £10,000.

Be prepared for a potential purchase to fall through. Often you may have to pay for more than one survey and extra legal fees. (For a breakdown of costs, see Table 5.)

Table 4: How the cut in MIRAS will affect monthly mortgage bills

Size of loan	Tax relief 15%	Tax relief 10%
Repayment		
£35,000	£243.23	£253.23
£55,000	£399.36	£409.36
£75,000	£555.49	£565.49
Endowment (interest only)		
£35,000	£203.24	£213.34
£55,000	£336.67	£346.67
£75,000	£470.00	£480.00

Source: Halifax – assuming a 25-year mortgage and interest rates of 8 per cent.

Stamp Duty

This is a tax that has to be paid on property costing over £60,000 and is charged at 1 per cent of the total purchase price (not just the proportion above £60,000). It rises to 1.5 per cent on properties over £250,000 and 2 per cent on those above £500,000. So if you buy a property that is less than £60,000 you pay no stamp duty. But on a property worth £100,000 you will pay £1000.

£ CASH TIP £

If the price you are paying is just more than one of these bands you can agree a purchase price in the lower stamp duty band with a separate figure for curtains, carpets and other fixtures and fittings.

Table 5: Typical costs of buying a home

Purchase price	£50,001	£100,001
Stamp Duty	Nil	£1,000
Legal fees	£441	£881
Local Search	£50	£50
Land Registry	£100	£230
MIG on 95 per cent mortgage	£800	£1,600
Mortgage Valuation	£145	£180
TOTAL	£1,536	£3,941

Source: Abbey National
NB: This excludes survey fees.

Legal Fees

There are three alternatives:

1   employ a solicitor

2   employ a licensed conveyancer

3   do your own conveyancing

Conveyancing fees are usually on a fixed basis. However, you may have to pay for extra services on top of this amount and VAT will be added. Always agree fees in advance. They tend to rise for homes worth more. Fees have dropped significantly to less than 1 per cent, so it is rarely worth your while to do your own conveyancing.

Searches

One of the solicitor or conveyancer's jobs is to do local searches to check that there are no plans in the pipeline that may affect the value or future of the home that you are buying. Local searches are charged on a flat fee basis and usually cost around £50. However, if you live in area that may need an extra geological search – for instance if there has been extensive mining in the past – this will cost extra.

Land registry fees

The solicitor or conveyancer will also register the transfer of ownership of the property into your name on the official register of land ownership called the Land Registry. The fees for this start at £40 and rise to £230 for a £100,000 to £150,000 property.

Survey Costs

In more than 80 per cent of purchases homebuyers buy without a thorough survey. They may pay tens or even hundreds of thousands of pounds for a home but are not prepared to pay a few hundred pounds on a survey. Unless you are buying a newly built or recently built home or a flat in a modern block, you should consider paying for a survey. If there is a major fault with the building this survey could save you thousands of pounds in the long run. Even if there are only minor faults a survey can still pay, as you may be able to negotiate a reduction in the asking price.

If you fail to have a survey not only will you have little idea of the amount of work that may be required, but also you may have no means of redress should you find that there are major problems.

Caveat Emptor – Or Buyer Beware

Agents – but not individuals – are obliged to be truthful when advertising and marketing properties under the Properties Misdescription Act 1991. This may give you some comfort. But if you are not relying on a survey but rather what the vendor tells you, you could be left seriously out of profit. Even estate agents are not obliged to disclose more than they feel like disclosing.

So if the estate agent knows there has been a negative survey that led to a potential buyer pulling out, that agent does not have to tell you. However, if you ask you must be told the truth. If the estate agent lies, he or she is breaking the law. However, if you ask the vendors and they lie, you will probably have no case.

Different Types of Survey

The valuation report

The cost is sometimes paid for by lender but is usually between £150 and £200. This is a very basic survey. Although you, as the buyer, must usually pay for it, it is designed to reassure the lender that the property is worth enough to cover the amount of the loan should you default on the mortgage repayments.

The valuation report will only outline any serious problems that affect the value of the property. So if the home is suffering from subsidence or damp this will be pointed out.

In a few cases the valuer may value the property at less than the asking or agreed purchase price. As a result, the amount the lender is prepared to lend may be reduced.

If major or substantial repairs are required on the property, the lender may withhold a proportion of the mortgage until these works have been completed. Often a time limit – say six months – is given in which these repairs or renovations must be carried out.

The homebuyers' survey and valuation

This costs between £300 and £400. It is more detailed than the valuation report and is often completed at the same time as the valuation and by the same surveyor. However, it is not what is commonly referred to as a 'full survey'. It is also known as the House Purchase and Valuation Report, the Homebuyers' Survey and Valuation (HBSV), or a Scheme Two Survey.

The survey is completed on a standard form and is designed to pick up major faults. The survey will also tell you if there are any items of work that you will need to complete shortly after moving in. Although the report should point out any damp, woodrot or woodworm, the surveyor will probably not inspect under floorboards or in the roof.

Building or full structural survey

This costs upwards of £400. It is recommended for those buying older properties, conversions of older properties, and unusual homes. It can be combined with the valuation although is often done separately.

You can usually save money by combining the valuation and full survey, provided that the surveyor is on the lender's approved panel. If you have any particular concerns, point these out to the surveyor and ask for a more detailed inspection. Put your request in writing so that if a fault appears after you have moved in you can claim redress from the surveyor.

New homes

If you are buying a new property or a recently built home it will probably be covered by a ten year warranty. These are issued when homes are first built but are transferred to new owners if the house is sold within the warranty period.

The main warrant is the one offered by the National House Building Council (NHBC).

If you are buying a newer home you may feel that you can dispense with a survey. However, one may still be advisable if the warranty is nearing its end. The warranty scheme only covers *all* defects with the property for the first two years, but for the remaining eight years it merely covers major damage due to structural defects.

Once You Have Taken Out a Mortgage

Is It Worth Switching Your Mortgage?

Once you have taken out a mortgage there is nothing to stop you switching to another lender to cut your monthly mortgage bills. The average homebuyer switches mortgage every seven years, usually because they move, but increasingly because borrowers switch to another, cheaper lender.

However, if you are locked into a discount or fixed rate mortgage you will be tied in for up to five years. If you want to switch you will probably have to repay the discount or pay a penalty of a percentage of your loan – often 5 per cent. So weigh up the options. If you will have to pay £500 in redemption penalties but will save £1000 or more in interest over two years you will be far better off switching.

£ CASH TIP £

If you complain about the rate you are paying, your lender may offer you a more competitive deal and in some cases banks and building societies have been known to make secret cash payments – sometimes amounting to hundreds of pounds – to persuade borrowers not to switch to rival lenders. You will not be offered these deals automatically, so it pays to complain.

Paying Off Your Mortgage Early

If you have spare cash or can afford higher monthly repayments you can make additional mortgage payments to reduce your mortgage. However, not all lenders make this easy. Some only allow additional payments once a year, and others require that you pay in a minimum additional amount. This can mean that although you make additional monthly repayments of £50 this is not credited to your mortgage account for several months because the minimum partial redemption is £500 – and you do not earn any interest on this cash. Before making an additional payment check the terms of your mortgage.

Warning: If you have a fixed rate or discount mortgage you may find that additional part-repayment triggers redemption penalties. So repaying £500 from your loan could cost you £1000 in penalties and yet save you only a minimal amount in monthly mortgage payments.

Potential Pitfalls

Joint Purchasing

The advantage of buying with a friend, partner or spouse is that you can borrow more money – usually three times the main salary, plus the other salary or two and half times joint income – and can split the costs. But if you fall out or one of you wishes to sell and the other does not want to move you could find that one of you cannot afford to buy out the other owner. Even married couples face a high risk, with one in three marriages ending in divorce.

A straightforward repayment loan may be better than an endowment mortgage in these cases, as you will not be forced to sell your endowment (which will mean that you suffer early surrender values) and it is easy to work out how much has been paid and how much is owing.

The alternative is to take out separate endowment policies. However, if one party dies the endowment will only cover half of the loan so an additional term life insurance policy may be necessary. Some insurers offer twin-plan endowment schemes that give separate endowment policies but joint life cover.

Types of joint ownership

If you are buying a property with another person you have two choices:

1   Joint tenancies are the most common. Each person is assumed to own half the equity and if one partner dies the other inherits that person's share of the property, irrespective of what their will says.

2   Tenancy in common, the legal alternative, allows for varying financial arrangements. If you draw up a trust

deed you can set down exactly how much each person has invested in the home. So if one partner has paid a bigger share of the deposit or pays more towards the mortgage, the deed enables the buyers to agree at the outset what will happen to the property should the relationship break down. Tenancy in common allows each of the owners to leave their share of the property in their will as they wish.

Leaseholds

If you are buying a leasehold property with a short lease you may not be able to get a mortgage as lenders generally require leases to be for at least sixty years.

Warning: Always allow for increases in service charges on leasehold properties when budgeting for what you can afford. Service charges can spiral if they are only reviewed every few years or if the building needs extensive repairs. That is why it is essential to a have a survey on older blocks of flats. Remember, you will be liable for a proportion of the costs of replacing the roof, repointing the brickwork, or repairing any other problems.

If You Lose Your Job

All mortgages taken out after 1 October 1995 have different benefit rules and you will not normally be entitled to government assistance for the first nine months following redundancy. It therefore makes sense to take out your own protection policy.

Cashing in your endowment

Homebuyers who fall into arrears often find that they cannot pay their endowment premiums. Always check if there are financial penalties for suspending payments. If you are tempted to cash in your endowment policy, remember that you will generally require the consent of your lender and the amount you receive will be cut by early-surrender penalties. The alternative is to sell your endowment, as you can generally receive more than from surrendering it. The Association of Policy Market Makers will supply lists of companies that offer this service (0171 739 3949). Only with-profits endowments or whole-of-life with-profits policies can be sold on the second-hand market. This is because they already have a value that cannot be taken away. If you sell your policy you can receive between 15 and 40 per cent more for your policy than you would receive as a surrender value. Alternatively, if your endowment policy is in surplus you may be able to borrow against it.

9 *Insurance*

It is better to be safe than sorry.

Although this chapter is near to the end of this book, its subject is not something that should be left to last. Insurance is essential to protect your home, car, life and income.

As with most financial products it pays to shop around. Intense competition and new entrants into the market have increased choice for the consumer. However, the only way to gain from this is by being aware of what is on offer.

Most insurers rely on apathy and expect customers to renew their policies automatically. But just because a policy was the best value last year does not mean it is still good value this year. Insurers are also offering no claims bonuses on a range of insurance products – not just motor insurance – to encourage customer loyalty.

Insurance premium tax is currently charged at 4 per cent on most general insurance policies, but could rise. There is a higher rate of tax on insurance sold with goods or services, particularly travel insurance, which is taxed at 17.5 per cent from a travel agent but only 4 per cent if bought separately.

Direct Insurance Companies

To get the best insurance deals you have to be the best risk. The introduction of 'direct' insurers offering cheap insurance over the telephone has led to 'cherry picking' of the best customers. This means that if you are a poorer risk – a younger driver or a householder who has made past burglary claims or lives in a high-crime area – you may find cover expensive or refused. Although this goes against the object of insurance – to spread the costs of a few among many – it does make insurance cheaper for some.

Buildings and Contents Insurance

These two types of insurance are covered together as generally they are bought as a package. However, there is nothing to stop you from shopping around and buying them separately to save on costs. But be aware that should you have to make a claim you may have to deal with two insurance companies and there may be problems in agreeing which insurer covers what.

Your bank or building society may require that you take out buildings and contents insurance as a condition of the loan, so you may have no choice. If not, your lender may still encourage you to take out insurance with an insurance company it owns or is tied to.

One recent survey found that homeowners who buy their buildings and contents insurance through their mortgage lender are paying up to 78 per cent more than they need to. If you want to switch to a cheaper alternative you will probably be charged for administration – usually £25. But it may still be worth shopping around as you could easily save £100 a year and often your new insurer will refund the £25 administration fee.

What Affects Costs

Amount of cover

Buildings: This is the cost of rebuilding _not_ the market valuation. The rebuild cost is usually determined at the time of purchase and then rises in line with inflation in building costs. If you have purchased a flat the insurance will generally be included as part of your service charges.

Cover includes: the fabric of your home – bricks and mortar, windows, roof, floors, and anything that is a fixture or fitting such as your kitchen units, built-in wardrobes and doors. You are insured against theft, fire, storms (but not damage to fences or hedges), flood and subsidence.

Buildings cover starts at about £1.30 for every £1000 insured but can rise to as much as £4 per £1000.

£ CASH TIP £

Rebuild costs are usually less than the market valuation. If you think you are insured for too much you can ask a surveyor to value your property for insurance purposes. Some combination policies are rated on the number of bedrooms to save you from seeking an accurate rebuild figure. The Association of British Insurers (0171 600 3333) produces a leaflet to help you check that your bedroom-rated policy provides the right amount of cover.

Warning: If you do not insure your property for enough – either initially or because you have not increased your cover following extensive improvements – your insurer will probably not meet your claim in full.

Contents: This is either the value of the contents or cover is based on the number of rooms or bedrooms in your property. Cover is for everything that is not a fixture or fitting and can even include belongings lost or stolen if they are temporarily taken out of the home.

£ CASH TIP £

Do not underinsure. Either accurately value all your contents (do not forget to include carpets, curtains, clothes, books, groceries and toiletries) or opt for a policy that covers your size of property.

£ CASH TIP £

Make a list of all your contents and keep it up-to-date and in a safe place. Should the worst happen, and you lose all your belongings in a fire or they are damaged by flood, you will find it difficult to remember exactly what you owned. Keeping receipts is always a good idea – even if only to return goods should they be faulty. They can also help support an insurance claim.

Warning: Some policies have a maximum limit on the value of individual items. This can mean that valuables are not covered by your policy and they may have to be insured separately or for an additional or higher premium. Get valuables professionally valued for insurance purposes.

Type of cover

The cheapest policies do not pay out for the full replacement value of items that are stolen or destroyed and only give you the second-hand value. These are not a good idea. If your property were to burn to the ground and you had to replace everything you would be left out of pocket. You will be better off with 'new-for-old', which gives you the replacement value.

At the more expensive end of the spectrum a policy can also cover:

▌ accidental damage to your contents (and should be considered for buildings as it will cover a foot through the ceiling while you are in the loft)

▌ all risks, which covers belongings, including cash, taken out of the home

---

Warning: Always read the small print on your policy as you may find that some items are excluded such as bicycles or the contents of your garden shed.

Level of risk

You will pay more if you live in an area (usually determined by post code) that has a high number of burglaries or is more prone to subsidence. However, you can reduce the risks and therefore the costs of insurance. The following usually enable householders to claim a discount on their premiums:

▌ Increase your home's security devices – fit window locks and a burglar alarm.

▌ Join (or set up) a neighbourhood watch scheme.

▌ In some cases double glazing is also classed as a burglar deterrent.

E. Wright & Co. (Insurances)

Lyndon House, 49 Lyndon Road,
Sutton Coldfield, West Midlands B73 6BS
Telephone: 0121 321 2717 Fax: 0121 321 2718

In the world of Finance and Investment there are so many conflicting views and opinions. How best can you decide on the correct path for you to take?

The answer is simple. Take advantage of the services of a truly Independent Financial Adviser. There are many to choose from so why us?

We have been well established in the area since 1980. The Principal, Mr E E Wright, has well over 30 years experience in Financial Planning. Others in the industry have come and gone but we continue to grow from strength to strength. Not least because we place paramount importance on offering sound ethical advice. When we select insurance companies and investment houses with which to deal, we place great emphasis on a proven track record.

Our areas of expertise as an Independent Financial Adviser are:-

1) All forms of Life Assurance

2) Pensions both for the employed and self employed

3) Investments including wide ranging P.E.P.s

4) Critical Illness and Income Protection

5) Private Health care provision

6) Sound advice on house purchase, ie the correct mortgage and procedures
   necessary to ensure a hassle free transaction.

*Finally, our separate general insurance department can deal
with all aspects of general, household and motor insurances.*

▓   Do you have someone at home all day? This reduces the risks of burglary and therefore your insurance premiums.

Likewise, if the risks to the insurer are higher – you have made a claim in the recent past or you live in a high-risk area – your premiums are also likely to cost more.

Warning: Some insurers require a minimum level of security – five-bar mortice locks on the front door and window locks – before they will provide you with cover.

The excess

This is the amount that you pay towards a claim – say the first £500 or £2000. The higher the excess the lower the premiums.

Switching Insurers

If you are in an area that is at risk from subsidence you may have a problem should you need to claim after you have switched insurers, as your new insurance company may claim that some of the damage was caused before you switched policies. However, a recent agreement among insurers should mean that this is now less of a problem.

Problems Making a Claim

A recent *Which? Magazine* survey found that one in seven people had their claim down-valued by their insurer.

Why a claim may be reduced

Wear and tear: Most policies pay out sufficient to replace your damaged or stolen goods with new items. These are known as 'new-for-old' policies. However, in some cases the insurer may make a deduction for 'wear and tear' and only give you the second-hand value. This can sometimes include bed linen.

You have not met the policy terms and conditions: If your policy requires that you fit five-bar mortice locks on your door and you fail to use these you could find that your insurer is reluctant to meet your burglary claim. Likewise, if you fail to lock your bicycle and it is stolen you have failed to meet the policy's conditions.

You do not have sufficient cover: If you have insured your building for only 80 per cent of its rebuilding value you cannot expect the insurance company to pay for all the rebuilding costs. Contents insurance claims can also be scaled down in this way.

Repair rather than replacement: In some cases the insurance company may insist that damaged items are repaired rather than replaced. In this case make sure that the repairs return the item to its original state, and follow the procedures for getting quotes from repair firms or else the insurer may claim that the costs are too high.

Insurance Investigations

In some cases – particularly if you are making a large or unusual claim – the insurance company will send round a loss adjuster to examine your insurance claim. This does not mean that the insurance company thinks your claim is fraudulent. However, the loss adjuster will check that your claim is genuine, that you have met the terms and conditions of your insurance policy, and that you are claiming a reasonable amount. You do not pay the loss adjuster's fees – these are met by the insurance company.

Even if the adjuster reduces the size of the claim, you can dispute this if you think this is unfair. To ensure you receive the maximum insurance payout (particularly for major claims) you can employ a loss assessor.

Motor Insurance

The chances are that as young professional you will have two particular risk factors increasing your premiums – your age and the fact that you live in an urban area.

One in four motor insurance policies is now arranged over the telephone so you will not see any paperwork until after you have bought the cover. Read this carefully.

You are under a legal duty to disclose every single material fact when applying for a policy or renewing one. If you do not the insurance company can repudiate the policy completely. But you may not know what facts you should have disclosed so read the exclusion clauses carefully.

What Type of Cover

Third-party fire and theft is the minimum cover required by law. However, it will not cover accidental damage to your car, and if someone else damages your car and then drives off you could be left with a write-off but no compensation. This type of cover should only be an option if you have a cheap old 'banger' that costs as much to insure as it does to buy. Even if you take out third-party, fire and theft cover you should ideally get a policy with uninsured loss recovery – you can buy this for an extra fee of between £12 and £15. It means that if the other party involved in an accident refuses to co-operate with his or her insurer and you have a legitimate claim, solicitors will handle the dispute for no extra costs.

Fully comprehensive is supposed to cover all liability. However, there can still be exclusions so read the policy wording carefully. Many policies exclude cover when your car is being used in the course of your employment. Travelling to and from work will be covered but not driving on company business.

DAILY TELEGRAPH LIFEPLANNER SERIES

Your First Home

BUYING, RENTING, SELLING AND DECORATING

Niki Chesworth

Tackles the whole range of issues the first time buyer or tenant will encounter. It addresses contractual issues, maintenance, decorating, legal problems and much more to provide the reader with all they need when renting or buying their first home.

£8.99 Paperback 160 pages ISBN 0 7494 2529 6
Order ref: KT529   Published: November 1997

How to Manage Your Career, Family and Life

Cary Cooper and Suzan Lewis

Looks at the practical, financial and emotional problems faced by any dual-career couple or family. It tackles issues like working from home, childcare, house-keeping, spending time together and much more.

£8.99 Paperback 160 pages ISBN 0 7494 2528 8
Order ref: KT528   Published: November 1997

The Young Professionals Guide to Personal Finance

Niki Chesworth

Consultancy fees are beyond the purses of young professionals, who have a practical attitude to finance and want to spend their money wisely. This book offers sound, impartial advice for their present situation and indicates the choices available. The author suggests how to plan for the future: marriage, mortgage, tax issues, using an accountant, pension planning, and making a will.

£8.99 Paperback 160 pages ISBN 0 7494 1961 X • Order ref: KS961   Published: November 1997

Cutting the Costs

Motorists spend an average £376 a year on car insurance but it easy to cut your bill by shopping around. Bear in mind the following:

▓ Younger drivers cost more to insure. Younger drivers are more likely to claim on their policy so insurers charge them more. If you have passed an advanced driving test you will normally qualify for a discount on your insurance premiums.

£ CASH TIP £

New young drivers are twice as likely to have an accident during their first year on the roads than other drivers. A new government-backed scheme called Pass Plus involves taking an extra six lessons. The insurance discounts should more than compensate for the £80 costs. One insurer gives a 30 per cent discount to those aged 21 to 24 who take the extra courses. Discounts can last for up to three years. For further information on Pass Plus call 0115 955 7736.

▓ No-claim bonuses reward careful drivers who do not make claims. The maximum is either a 60 or 65 per cent discount on your insurance premiums, which normally requires five years of making no claims to achieve. If you have built up a no-claims discount with another insurer this will normally be taken into account, and there may be a small discount if you were a company car driver that made no claims. You are under obligation to report all damage to your car – even if you do not want to make a claim – and this can reduce your no-claims discount. In many cases drivers are tempted to pay for low-cost repairs themselves and not report any damage to protect their no-claims bonus.

£ CASH TIP £

Take out an additional insurance policy to protect your no-claims discount. As a younger driver your premiums are likely to be higher and therefore the discount will be worth more.

£ CASH TIP £

If you have been a company car driver or a named driver on another person's motor insurance policy, find an insurer that will take your clean record into account and offer you a partial or full no-claims bonus.

▉ **Security:** If you keep your car in a garage or off the road overnight and have extra security devices you may get a discount.

▉ **The policy excess:** This is the amount you must pay towards each claim. Often the driver must pay the first £100 to £500. If you opt for a higher excess your premiums will be lower.

▉ **Your occupation:** Some insurers penalize those in certain occupations while others specialize in giving certain occupations a discount. Ask an insurance broker for advice.

Warning: If belongings are stolen from your car they may not be covered, or there may be an overall maximum of a relatively low amount – say £150 – for car contents.

£ CASH TIP £

Ask your household insurer if it offers dicsounts to take out additional policies including car insurance.

£ CASH TIP £

If you insure someone else on your car insurance policy it could cost you far more. However, if you include your spouse on your cover it can actually be cheaper, as some companies see married couples as a safer risk.

£ CASH TIP £

Pay your premium in full rather than in monthly instalments and you will often qualify for a discount of up to 10 per cent.

Making a Claim

Always follow the procedures set down by your insurer.

Your policy may require you to use recommended repairers or to get three quotations before any work can begin. If you do not follow these rules you may have to pay all or part of the repair costs yourself.

The Motor Insurance Bureau (telephone 01908 240 000) was set up to sort out claims where the party at fault is uninsured or untraceable (in some parts of the country as many as one in ten motorists drives without insurance). Just because someone refuses to report an accident does not prevent you from claiming. The MIB then becomes responsible.

Life Insurance

If you are young and have no dependants, you may not feel you need life insurance and you may be right. However, you will need to buy cover – either term assurance or an endowment policy – if you take out a mortgage. And even though you may not need life cover now you will find that it is cheaper if you take it out at an earlier age.

Those with no dependants may be better off opting for insurance that pays out if they are injured (accident insurance) or fall ill and are unable to look after themselves or earn a living (critical illness or permanent health insurance). These are covered later in this chapter.

The different forms of life insurance include:

Term assurance: This is bought for a fixed term and pays out a fixed sum during the term of the policy or occasionally a rising level of cover. At the end of the policy term you receive nothing back. This is the cheapest form of life insurance and if you buy it through your pension (up to 5 per cent of premiums can be spent on life cover) you will get tax relief on your premiums. The older you are when you take out this policy, then generally the more expensive the premiums.

£ CASH TIP £

Although premiums tend to be low you can still cut costs by shopping around. There is no penalty if you cancel a policy. If your policy is linked to your mortgage, check with your lender before switching policies.

Whole of life: This is part investment and part life cover. As the name implies it pays out at any time during your life as long as you pay the premiums or until the policy term is finished. If you are expecting returns similar to an endowment, do not be mislead. Whole of life premiums mainly buy life cover and hardly any is invested.

Endowments: These are mainly an investment but they do have an element of life cover (usually sufficient to repay a mortgage). How endowments work is explained in Chapter 8.

Life Insurance Shares

When financial institutions such as building societies and life insurance companies convert from mutual status they offer shares to investors. The Norwich Union has already paid out free shares, and others tipped to convert include Equitable Life. Not only can investors gain from investing but they also have the potential to earn shares or bonuses on conversion. But do not pick a policy in the hope of receiving free shares. You should still opt for the most suitable policy to meet your needs. However, check that your type of policy qualifies for free shares.

Private Medical Insurance

Some 6 million have private medical insurance and of these some 60 per cent are within company schemes. The remainder include a large number of self-employed. While only 11 per cent of the population are covered by insurance, some 20 per cent of all operations are carried out privately and 30 per cent of minor operations. In these cases patients opt to pay the medical bills rather than the soaring costs of private medical insurance, which are rising by 10 to 15 per cent a year – well above inflation.

Increasingly insurers are offering budget-priced and cutdown plans. But in exchange for lower premiums you will have lower cover. These policies often exclude outpatient treatment, provide cover only for certain illnesses, or ask policyholders to pay towards their annual treatment costs.

If you are offered private medical insurance as a perk of employment then you will pay tax on the cost to your employer. So if the cost is £180 a year and you are a 40 per cent taxpayer you will pay 40 per cent of £180, that is £72, in tax.

Remember private medical insurance does not cover accidents and emergencies or any pre-existing or chronic medical conditions. It is for conditions that may take a long time to be treated on the NHS or you want dealt with quickly and in a private hospital.

Check what is covered, if it is covered in full, and if there are any limits on the amount you can claim for each type of cover (including surgeons' fees), and remember that there will usually be restrictions on where you can be treated.

Warning: If your medical bills are higher than the agreed rate set by your health insurer you could find that you have to pay extra bills even though you think you are fully covered.

Ways to reduce the costs

Some policies now offer no-claims discounts that can start at 25 per cent if you do not make a claim for a year, and can increase to up to 50 per cent.

Other policies are cheaper because they only cover you if you are not treated on the NHS within a certain time period – often within six weeks.

Some policies also have high excesses. One insurer has cut premiums by up to 90 per cent but in return customers have to agree to pay the first £4000 of any claim. However, in many cases claims do not exceed this.

Insuring Your Income

There are several ways to insure your financial health, from payment protection insurance to permanent health cover.

Critical illness and permanent health insurance are aimed at those who would suffer financial problems if they could not work – those running their own businesses, the self-employed and freelancers. They will also appeal to those who are single and may not have need for a life insurance policy but who may need a lump sum to pay for nursing help and care if they contract a serious illness.

A few policies are a cross between permanent health insurance (PHI) and critical illness cover (CIC).

Costs

These depend on:

■ your age

■ sex

■ if you smoke

■ medical history

■ occupation

▓ amount insured

▓ term

▓ illnesses covered

▓ benefits

Critical Illness Insurance

Critical illness pays out if you contract one of a limited range of diseases, usually a serious and normally life-threatening illness. Payment is a lump sum and is paid out regardless of the severity of the illness and whether or not you recover. Payment does not normally start until 28 days after diagnosis, so if you have a terminal heart attack you will not receive a penny. These policies are designed to help those living with an illness rather than dying from one. Cancer, heart attack, stroke, kidney failure, major organ transplant, and coronary artery bypass surgery are covered. Multiple sclerosis and a few other illnesses can also be included. Most policies will also cover you for total and permanent disability (TPD), even if this is caused by something not specifically listed on the policy. However, always read the small print carefully as the definitions vary.

Critical illness cover is often combined with other financial products such as an endowment linked to your mortgage or your life insurance policies. However, if you combine CIC with life insurance after diagnosis of a critical illness your could use up your entire fund in paying for care and then have no money in the fund to pay for life insurance cover. If you keep your two policies separate you will get critical illness payments while you need care and a lump-sum life insurance payment for your dependants.

CIC combined with your endowment is designed to pay off your mortgage but will not provide you with any additional payment. However it is cheaper – between £5 and £8 on top of a £50,000 endowment policy for a 29-year-old man.

Premiums may seem high so these policies will appeal only to those who know that they would suffer great financial difficulty if they could not work. However, the chances of your needing to claim are high. Men have a one in four chance of developing a serious illness before 65 and women a one in five chance.

Watch out for the small print. For instance, some policies cover loss of limb if your arm is severed above the wrist or your leg above the ankle but other policies require that both limbs be severed above either the elbow or knee.

The same applies with permanent disability. Some policies pay out if you are unable to work, whereas others require that you have lost mobility and cannot dress or feed yourself.

If you enjoy mountaineering, flying your own aeroplane or other dangerous pursuits or are injured because of alcohol or drug abuse the policy is unlikely to pay out. One-fifth of claims are rejected, so you must be aware of your policy terms and conditions. Also, ensure that you disclose all details of your past medical history on your application form or else your claim may be rejected.

Permanent Health Insurance

Permanent health insurance protects your income and covers you for a wider range of diseases and illnesses than critical illness insurance, including back pain if it means you cannot work. Instead of paying out a lump sum, the policy pays out an agreed level of income. Once you are fit to work again, you no longer receive any payment. There is usually a delay (often a month or more) before the policy starts to pay out and there are usually strict restrictions on who can get cover and there will probably be exclusions for past medical complaints.

Critical illness cover is cheaper than PHI, which is probably why more people are opting for the former. However, in many cases PHI will suit your needs better and it also covers more illnesses. If you are only worried that you will not have enough income to pay your monthly mortgage repayments, consider mortgage payment protection insurance as this is cheaper.

Payment Protection Insurance

This is usually bought when you take out a credit card, loan or mortgage. It either pays your monthly repayments or will repay the entire debt if you lose your job or can no longer earn an income due to ill health. However, the policy terms and conditions can be restrictive and may not cover the self-employed and could require that you have remained in the same job for a certain period of time (so if you move jobs you could invalidate your insurance). Read the small print carefully.

If you have several payment protection policies for your credit cards, mortgages, hire purchase agreements, etc, you can take out one single policy. This may offer different or more comprehensive cover than the individual plans and you could cut the costs. Mortgage payment protection insurance is covered in Chapter 8.

Income Protection

An income protection plan provides an income should you be made redundant. The period over which the policy pays out can vary and there is often a set period before payments are made. There are often strict conditions.

Complaints About Insurance

Most insurance companies have complaints procedures. If you did not receive details of these along with your policy document ask the insurance company to send you details of how to complain.

Most major insurance companies are members of the Insurance Ombudsman Bureau but you can only take your case to the Ombudsman if you have exhausted your insurer's complaints procedure. The Ombudsman can make awards of up to £100,000 and these are binding on the insurance company. However, if you are not satisfied with the decision you can still take your case to court.

Some insurance companies are members of the Personal Insurance Arbitration Service (PIAS) instead of the Ombudsman scheme. However, unlike the Ombudsman's service, you need the insurer's consent to use it and once a decision has been made it is binding. This means that if you are unhappy with the ruling you cannot then pursue you case through the courts.

Contacts

The Association of British Insurers (0171 600 3333) produces fact sheets on different aspects of insurance.

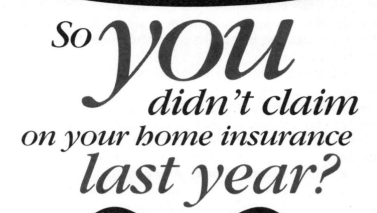

So *you* didn't claim on your home insurance *last year?*

Legal & General's home insurance cover rewards careful homeowners. So if you haven't claimed for a year or more – whoever you're insured with – you'll enjoy a no-claims discount of up to 20%. Why not call today for a no-obligation quote?

Lines open 8AM – 8PM weekdays, 9AM – 1PM Saturday

0800 32 42 52

Please quote reference 5631-7P when you call

Legal & General

 **Tax**

Nothing can be said to be certain except death and taxes.

Income Tax

If you are an employee you will be taxed at source, which means that the correct amount of tax should be deducted from your pay before you receive your wage cheque. This is collected by your employer and passed to the Inland Revenue under the Pay-As-You-Earn tax system.

However, it is still possible to pay too much – or too little – income tax if the Inland Revenue is unaware that your circumstances have changed.

Income Tax Rates and Tax Bands

Income tax is charged at three different tax rates on income that falls into different tax bands. You only pay each rate of tax on income that falls within a particular tax band. This means that you can pay tax at the three different rates if you have income in each of these tax bands. (See Table 6.)

Tax Allowances

You do not have to pay tax on all of your income. Everyone is entitled to a tax allowance. This is the amount that you

Table 6: Income tax rates and bands

Tax rate	%	Tax band for the year 6 April 1997 to 5 April 1998	Tax you will pay
Lower	20%	£1–£4,100	max £820
Basic	23%	£4,101–£26,100	max £5,880
Higher	40%	£26,101+	min £5,880

can earn before paying income tax. It is essential that you check that you have the right allowances (see Table 7).

▌ **Personal allowance:** Everyone is entitled to the personal allowance but you can only claim it once, so if you have more than one job or are an employee but also have additional earnings from self-employment, you can only set the personal allowance against once source of income – usually the main source of earnings.

▌ **Married couple's allowance:** If you are married and living with your spouse you are entitled to an additional allowance that is added to your personal allowance. If you marry after 5 April you will be entitled to one-twelfth of the married couple's allowance for each month of your marriage. The allowance is given to the husband. However, the wife can claim half the allowance without her husband's consent and all of the allowance with his agreement.

▌ **Single parent allowance:** If you are single, separated, divorced or widowed, and have a child living with you you can claim this allowance.

Table 7: Tax allowances for the tax year April 1997 to April 1998

Personal (under 65)	£4,045
Married couple's (under 65)	£1,830 (15% only)
Single parent's	£1,830 (15% only)

How allowances reduce your tax bill

Although the basic personal allowance is £4045 this is not the amount of tax you save. You only save the tax you would have had to pay on this amount of income. The savings depend on your top rate of tax. If you are a higher rate taxpayer the savings will be 40 per cent of £4045, that is to say £1618.

How tax allowances vary

Not all tax allowances save you tax at your highest rate. Some are restricted to a certain level of tax savings. The married couple's allowance is restricted to a 15 per cent tax saving. So if you qualify for the married couple's allowance you will only get a fixed amount of tax savings regardless of the rate of tax you pay. This is 15 per cent of £1830, that is to say £274.50.

£ CASH TIP £

If you marry during the tax year do not forget to claim your married couple's allowance. You can get a proportion of the allowance. So if you wed halfway through the year you are entitled to half the married couple's allowance.

Tax Codes

Employees who receive their salary under the PAYE (Pay-As-You-Earn) tax system will have a tax code.

This adjusts your tax allowances to collect any additional tax you may owe. So if you have any taxable employee benefits (such as a company car) your tax allowances will be lower than the basic personal tax allowance.

Your tax code is your responsibility and it is up to you – not the Inland Revenue or your employer – to check that your code is correct.

Where to find your tax code

You may have been sent a PAYE Coding Notice by the Inland Revenue. This will tell you what your tax code is. If you have not been sent one you should be able to find your tax code on your wage slip.

The code is made up of numbers (usually two or three) and a letter, for example 312H or K 311.

The figures in your code show the amount you can earn in the tax year before paying tax. When the Inland Revenue works out your Tax Code it deletes the last number. So if you can earn £2965 before paying tax your code will include the figures 295.

The letter next to your code tells your employer what type of taxpayer you are.

The most commonly used letters are:

L: You get the basic personal allowance – this code is normally given to single people with no employee benefits.

H: You are entitled to the basic personal allowance and the married couple's allowance. Again, this is normally given to those with no employee benefits.

T: Your tax code will be adjusted by the Inland Revenue not your employer. This is given to those who have employee perks that change in value on a regular basis.

K: You qualify for no personal allowance at all because the value of your employee benefits and other deductions is greater than your personal allowances. This means that you not only pay tax on all your income but an additional sum of tax will be deducted each month through PAYE so that you do not face a tax bill at the end of the year.

Checking your tax code

Add up all the personal allowances you are entitled to. This will usually be the personal allowance and the married couple's allowance.

If you are entitled to higher rate tax relief on personal pension contributions (employer schemes have this credited automatically) this tax relief should be added to your allowances.

Then add up all your deductions. You pay tax on your employee benefits (such as your company car) by an adjustment to your tax code. Any outstanding tax from previous tax years, tax you owe on savings interest, and other earnings can also be taxed by adjusting (reducing) your tax code.

Subtract these deductions from your allowances to work out the final figure. Remember that the married couple's allowance is restricted to 15 per cent so you cannot simply deduct the £1830 allowance.

Tax Paperwork

If you are an employee you will receive several important documents during the year that you must keep.

▌ **The P60 Certificate of Pay:** This shows you much you have earned and how much income tax and national insurance contributions have been deducted from your salary. You should be given this by your employer by 31 May each year.

▌ **The P11D or P9D:** This lists your employee benefits (such as your company car) and expenses paid to you during the tax year. This should be given to you by your employer by 8 July each year.

▌ **Tax Coding Notice:** This will be sent to you by the Inland Revenue if your tax code changes.

▌ **The P45 (Part 1 A):** If you move jobs this will be given to you by your former employer.

The Taxation of Employee Benefits

Employee benefits (also known as benefits-in-kind) are the perks that you are given as part of your remuneration package. These can include a company car, free petrol, private health insurance, a subsidised mortgage, and a mobile phone.

However, not all benefits are taxable. Some expenses – those that are incurred 'wholly, exclusively and necessarily' on behalf of your employer and purely for business – are tax exempt.

You pay tax on your employee benefits at the highest rate of tax you pay, and are taxed on the value of the perk. This is known as the cash equivalent. So if your perk has a taxable value (often the cost to your employer) of £1000, as a higher rate taxpayer you will pay a £400 tax.

In some cases you are taxed on a fixed amount regardless of how much the perk costs your employer. For instance, the cash equivalent or taxable value of mobile phones is fixed at £200. There are different rules for employees earning less than £8500 a year, however these are not explained here as it is unlikely that these will apply to readers of this book.

The Taxation of Company Cars

Company cars are taxed on 35 per cent of the list price at the time the car was registered. This value includes accessories. So if your car has a list price of £10,000 the taxable value or cash equivalent will be £3500. This is not the amount of tax you pay. If you are a higher rate taxpayer you will pay 40 per cent of £3500, that is to say £1400.

However, you may find that you pay less tax than this straight 35 per cent of value. This is because the tax is reduced for those who use their car for business rather than just as a perk. (See Table 8.)

Table 8: How company car tax can be reduced

Reason for car tax reduction	Amount of reduction
If you drive between 2500 and 18,000 business miles in the tax year	The taxable value of your car is reduced by one-third
If you drive more than 18,000 business miles in the tax year	The taxable value of your card is reduced by two-thirds
If your car was over four years old at the end of the tax year (5 April)	The taxable value of your car is reduced by one-third
If you pay your employer for private use of your company car	The taxable value is reduced by the amount you pay your employer
If you have use of the car for only part of the year	The taxable value is reduced proportionately

You do not pay tax on pool cars made available for business use. If you have a van made available for private use you pay tax on a £500 flat rate cash equivalent unless the car is over four years old, in which case the cash equivalent is £350.

£ CASH TIP £

If possible try to drive at least 2500 business miles a year to save on tax. If your car is to be renewed, consider one with a lower taxable value or not renewing the car at all (cars over four years old have a one-third reduction in the taxable value).

Free fuel from your company

If your employer pays you expenses for petrol or diesel for private use of your car you are taxed on this additional perk. You do not pay tax if the fuel is only provided for business journeys or you repay your employer in full (part payment towards the cost of fuel for private motoring will not reduce your tax bill). Remember you pay tax on the cash equivalent – this is not the amount of tax you pay. (See Table 9.)

Table 9: Fuel benefits – taxable benefit of petrol/diesel for private use of your company car (1997–98)

Engine size	Petrol	Diesel
1400cc or less	£800	£740
1401–2000cc	£1,010	£740
Over 2000cc	£1,490	£940

Reply today
and receive a
free
pen

To receive more information on any Legal & General products, simply complete this card and put it in the post (no stamp needed). In return, you will also receive a free Legal & General pen.

Surname _____
(Mr/Mrs/Miss/Ms/Other)
Forename(s) _____

Address _____

_____

_____ Postcode _____

Tel No. Home _____

Tel No. Work _____

Please send me more information on the following Legal & General products (please tick):

☐ Home contents insurance –
   my policy renewal date is   /   /

☐ Buildings insurance –
   my policy renewal date is   /   /

☐ Personal Pension Plan   ☐ Index-Tracking PEP

☐ Family Protection Plan   ☐ Flexible Reserve Mortgage

Now and then, we may tell you about other products or services offered by the Legal & General Group of companies that we believe may be of interest to you. If you would prefer not to receive this carefully selected information, please tick ☐.

**Legal &
General**

Signature(s) _____

Legal & General Direct Limited
FREEPOST (SWC1006)
CARDIFF
CF1 1YW

£ CASH TIP £

If you rarely use your company car for private journeys, consider paying your employer for the full cost of the private mileage. That way you escape the fuel benefit tax. However, if you use your car mainly for private usage you will be better off paying the tax. If your taxable benefit is £1010 you will pay £404 tax as a higher-rate taxpayer and £232.30 as a basic rate taxpyer. So if you spend £500 a year on petrol for private use you will be better off paying the tax (as this is lower) than paying the full price of the petrol.

Company car versus increased pay

Some companies give employees a choice of either a company car or an increase in salary. To calculate if this is worthwhile you must consider the following:

▪ Do I need a car? If you live near your place of work and do not need a car, take the pay.

▪ Will the additional salary cover the costs of buying another car?

▪ Will the additional salary also cover the extra costs of running a car? Most companies ensure company cars are regularly serviced, pay for insurance and road tax, and sign employees up to a roadside recovery service.

If your employer pays you expenses for using your own car

If your employer pays you for using your own car on company business, and you are paid a mileage allowance,

Table 10: Tax-free mileage allowances for 1997–98 for employees using their own car on company business

	Maximum reimbursement per mile	
Engine size	First 4000 business miles	Excess over 4000 business miles
Up to 1000cc	28p	17p
1001–1500cc	35p	20p
1501–2000cc	45p	25p
over 2000cc	63p	36p

this is tax free provided that it is within certain allowed limits. (See Table 10.)

You only have to pay tax if the mileage allowance you are paid exceeds these tax-free limits.

If your employer does not pay you a set amount per mile but instead reimburses you only for the fuel used on business journeys you can claim additional expenses including some of the running costs such as maintenance, insurance and road tax. These additional expenses can be reimbursed by your employer and are not taxable.

To do this you will need to keep exact records of business and private mileage. You can then tax deduct the business proportion. So if you drive 10,000 miles a year and 5000 of these are on business, you can claim half of your motoring costs.

You can also claim for some of the costs of buying the car such as interest on a loan. In addition, you can claim what are known as 'capital allowances' – a proportion of the costs of buying your car. You can only do this if you have not already claimed for running costs under the mileage allowance.

So if you buy a car to use partly for business and you drive 10,000 miles a year with 2000 of these exclusively for your job, you can claim 25 per cent of the cost of the car in the first year and then a further 25 per cent of the remainder every year thereafter.

Cost of buying the car = £10,000
Business proportion = $^1/_5$ (2000 miles out of 10,000)
So capital allowances can be claimed on £2000 of the purchase costs
Capital allowance in year 1 = 25% of £2000 = **£500**
Capital allowance in year 2 is 25% of the remaining or written down value
   £2000 – £500 = £1,500
   25% of £1500 = **£375**
Capital allowance in year 3 is 25% of the remaining or written down value
   £1500 – £375 = £1125
   25% if £1125 = **£281.25**

This calculation or writing down continues until the car is worthless, sold or you no longer use it for business. The maximum capital allowance that can be claimed is £3000.

These capital allowances can be claimed in addition to the interest paid on loans you take out to buy a car that you then use on company business. The business proportion of interest can be deducted in the first four years of the loan.

Other Employee Benefits

Mobile phones

The taxable cash equivalent of these is £200. So a 40 per cent taxpayer will pay £80 tax each year. However, if you pay your employer for the full cost of private calls you do not have to pay tax.

Private medical or dental insurance

The taxable cash equivalent is generally the actual cost to your employer.

Subsidized mortgages

You are taxed on the difference between what the loan would have cost you if you had to take the loan from a lender and the actual amount you pay in interest. You usually still qualify for mortgage interest tax relief.

Self-assessment and Tax Returns

It is now even more important that you keep on top of your tax affairs than ever before. A new way of administering tax was introduced in April 1997. Called 'self-assessment', it shifted more responsibility on to the individual taxpayer and introduced fines for those who fail to complete their tax return on time.

Only one in three income tax payers has to fill in a tax return (they are sent out in April each year). Generally, if you are not sent a tax return you do not need to fill one in. However, it is up to you as the taxpayer to make sure you receive a tax return and not up to the Inland Revenue to send you one. You will usually be sent a tax return if you:

▪ are self-employed

▪ have more than one source of income

▪ are a higher rate tax payer needing to pay extra tax on savings

▪ need to claim higher rate tax relief on your personal pension contributions

■ have substantial investments

■ have a range of taxable employee perks.

If you think you need to fill in a tax return but have not been sent one, ask the Inland Revenue for advice. Your employer will be able to tell you which tax office you should contact.

What Does Self-assessment Mean?

■ You can calculate your own tax bill if you want to – although you do not have to.

■ All tax returns must be filed by 31 January – nine months after the end of the tax year on 5 April.

■ If you want the Inland Revenue to calculate your tax bill for you, you must submit your completed tax return by 30 September – just over five months after the end of the tax year.

■ You must pay your tax bill by 31 January – nine months after the end of the tax year. This is the same deadline for sending back your completed tax return if you want to calculate your own tax bill or pay an accountant to do it for you.

■ If you have substantial investment income, have freelance or consultancy earnings in addition to your main employment income, rent out a property, or are self-employed, you may also have to make interim tax payments. These are due on 31 January in the tax year and 31 July after the end of the tax year. These interim payments are known as payments 'on account'.

What Does Self-assessment Require You to Do?

▨ You must keep records of all your earnings, investments, income and tax.

▨ You must keep these financial documents for at least 22 months after the end of the the tax year to which they relate.

▨ If you fail to keep adequate records to support your tax return you could by fined up to £3000 by the Inland Revenue.

▨ You must let the Inland Revenue know if your circumstances change, for instance if you start earning money from self-employment or begin renting out a property. This is so the Inland Revenue can send you a tax return or the correct additional pages in your tax return.

What If I Fail to Meet the Requirements?

In the past, those who failed to file their tax return on time or were late paying their tax bill were rarely fined. The only financial penalty was interest charged on outstanding tax. But as from 31 January 1998 the new self-assessment system means that you will be fined. (See Table 11.)

The Inland Revenue has a free self-assessment helpline (0645 000 444) that operates out of office hours.

Capital Gains Tax

As only 75,000 people pay this each year, most readers will not have to pay this tax. But if you fail to plan ahead you could find that you are needlessly liable for capital gains tax.

Table 11: Fines imposed for non-completion of tax returns

Deadline	Fine/Penalty
Tax returns not sent back by 31 January	£100
Tax returns not sent back by 31 July	a further £100 fine
Tax returns still outstanding after this date	fines of up to £60 a day
Tax not paid by 31 January	Interest of 8.5% (subject to variation in line with interest rate changes)
Tax not paid by 28 February	5% surcharge
Tax still not paid by 31 July	10% surcharge

You pay capital gains tax if you sell or dispose of an asset – a possession, investment, share or a business – and you make a profit or gain. You pay the tax on the profit you make, _not_ the amount you receive when you sell an asset.

You make a gain if the value of something you have sold during a tax year (from 6 April to 5 April) has risen since you bought it and the profits of _all_ assets sold exceed the tax threshold. As with income tax, you are allowed to earn a certain amount tax free. Each year you can make £6500 of profits tax free – this is the 1997–98 threshold and it usually rises every year. This allowance covers the gains on all assets and is not per asset. You only pay capital gains tax on profits made above this allowance and you will be taxed at your top rate of tax.

Assets liable to capital gains tax include:

▓ land (apart from the grounds of your home if they are smaller than one and a quarter acres)

▓ shares and other share-based investments

▓ second homes

▓ antiques and works of art (unless they are chattels – see list below)

▓ unit and investment trusts

▓ most things you hold for personal or investment purposes unless they are exempt from capital gains tax.

Assets exempt from capital gains tax regardless of the profit you make on their sale, include:

▓ your main home provided you have not let it out or used it for business

▓ private cars

▓ personal possessions or chattels (which are each worth £6000)

▓ income or proceeds from Personal Equity Plans (PEPs)

▓ bonuses and interest added to TESSA accounts

▓ gilts – UK Government stocks and some corporate bonds

▓ life insurance policies (with some exceptions – mainly purchasing from a third party or another person, not the life insurance company)

▌ National Savings Investments

▌ inheritances – however, if at a later date you sell an inheritance you may still be liable to capital gains tax on any profits.

▌ any wasting assets – ones that had a predictable life of 50 years or less when they were acquired.

How to Work Out if You Have Made a Taxable Gain

To work out if you are liable for capital gains tax you must add up the total profit made on the disposal of all taxable assets in the tax year which runs from 6 April to 5 April.

Take the amount you received on the sale of the asset and then deduct:

▌ the price you paid for the asset or its value at the time it was given to you

▌ costs incurred in buying and selling the asset – stock-brokers fees, etc

▌ costs of enhancing the value of the asset – restoration, etc

▌ inflation – the Inland Revenue can supply details of how much you can deduct; this is known as the indexation allowance and means you do not have to pay capital gains tax if your profit is entirely due to inflation.

If You Make a Loss

You can set losses (when you dispose of an asset that has fallen in value) against gains in the current, future or past tax years, either to reduce or to eliminate your capital gains tax bill.

How to Avoid Paying Capital Gains Tax

The easiest way is to invest in tax-free schemes such as Personal Equity Plans (PEPs).

You should also try to use up your capital gains tax allowance whenever possible. You can do this by selling assets in part so that you do not make a massive profit in one tax year or by selling assets every year so you never make a taxable profit.

If you do not want to sell your investments you can use up your capital gains tax allowance by using a tax avoidance system known as 'bed and breakfasting'. This enables you to sell shares, unit or investment trusts at the very end of one tax year to use up your capital gains tax allowance, and then buy back the same assets the next day at the start of a new tax year. Your stockbroker, investment adviser or unit trust or investment trust company should be able to tell you how to do this cheaply.

Maximizing Your Earnings

Managing your personal finances means more than simply keeping an eye on your bank balance, saving and investing. You must also ensure that you are being paid in the most tax-efficient manner and that you make the right choices when it comes to career and pay.

In addition to your basic salary there are other ways of being remunerated, some of which are tax free or can turn out to be more lucrative.

Profit-related pay: Although this is now being phased out and will no longer run after the year 2000, if you are offered this it is worth considering. You can receive up to £4000 or a fifth of your pay (whichever is the lower) tax free. It is being phased out from a maximum of £4000 in 1997 to £2000 in 1998, £1000 in 1999, and to nil by the year 2000.

Profit sharing schemes: If your employer runs an approved profit sharing scheme you will receive a yearly tax-free allocation of shares (the maximum limit in value a year is the greater of £3000 or 10 per cent of annual salary subject to a ceiling of £8000). Provided you keep the shares until the end of the third year after allocation, the shares are tax free.

Buying Shares in Your Company

Save-As-You-Earn (SAYE) schemes: These offer employees the chance to buy shares in the company they work for at a discount of up to 20 per cent on the price of the share on the date the option is granted. If the shares rise significantly before you buy them the profits will be even greater. You can save between £5 and £250 a month to buy these shares, usually after five years but sometimes three. These schemes are tax free and the only tax you may be liable to is capital gains tax when you sell the shares.

Company share-option plans: These give you the option to buy shares in your employer's company at less than the market value. Again, in most cases these share options are not taxable unless the total value of all shares granted to you (subject to options) is more than £30,000 at the time new options are granted.

Most of these schemes are restricted to middle and senior management and are more commonly known as executive share option schemes.

Under these schemes you do not pay income tax on the grant of the option (or any increase in the market value of the shares before you buy them), and can buy the shares between three and ten years after the option is granted.

Employment Tax Tips

▓ If you have to join a professional body in order to carry out your profession, you may be able to tax deduct subscriptions. Ask you professional body for advice on how much you can deduct.

▓ If you have to buy certain items of equipment in order to do your job – such as office equipment – you can often claim a proportion of the costs (known as a capital allowance) to reduce your tax bill. Ask your tax office for advice.

▓ If your company pays for further training that you need to do your job more effectively, you can receive this benefit tax free.

Other Tax Tips

▓ If you need to rent out a room in your property to help pay the mortgage, you can earn up to £4250 (for the 1997–98 tax year) of rent tax free. You can only have one lodger and the room must be furnished.

▓ Only one in every two hundred taxpayers claims the maximum tax relief on their pension fund contributions. Try to use up your relief by paying in additional lump sums and backdate your contributions to claim tax relief for past years. Higher rate taxpayers receive £400 in tax relief for every £1000 invested in their personal pension. This tax break may not last forever, so make the most of it while you can.

11 Complaining and the Law

The pen is mightier than the sword.

If you have not been involved in a consumer or legal dispute already you are bound to be at some time in the future, whether it is complaining about shoddy workmanship by a building firm or fighting to get a deposit returned from your landlord.

Legal bills can be prohibitively expensive and as such you should be aware of ways to finance a legal battle or to resolve it for a minimal cost.

Legal Expenses Insurance

This covers your legal bills should you be involved in a consumer dispute or need legal help to deal with an employment problem. You may be able to get this free as part of a trade body or union membership. Many home insurance and motoring insurance policies also offer either free or low-cost legal expenses insurance that is either included in the policy or can be bought separately. The type of legal disputes that are covered by the policy is often restricted and there may be a limit on the amount of legal fees that will be paid. There may also be a restriction on the type of advice given.

Free Legal Advice

Many professional and trade bodies and trade unions offer free legal advice helplines. These are often restricted to telephone advice. In some cases you may have to pay a annual premium in order to get access to legal advice whenever you want. There may be a restriction covering the amount of legal help you can receive – for instance £25,000 of legal fees. Check if you will be given help in writing legal letters, be represented in court, if the legal adviser will negotiate on your behalf, and on the qualifications of the legal adviser. Some credit card issuers, car breakdown companies, and banks and building societies also offer this service.

Mediation

Most commonly used for disputes between neighbours, mediation is non-binding and can only be entered into with mutual consent. These schemes are useful if your claim is for a sum greater than the small claims limit, as you can avoid hefty legal fees. There is usually a fee. Mediation UK (0117 904 6661) is the umbrella organization and it should provide you with details of mediation services.

Citizens' Advice Bureaux and Law Centres

These can help resolve disputes. You should find the addresses of these in your local telephone directory. Often, there may be a waiting list. There is no fee.

Ombudsmen

These cover industry sectors and settle disputes once you have exhausted a company's internal complaints procedure. Unlike arbitration schemes, you can usually take your case to court if you are unhappy with the Ombudsman's ruling.

These services are usually free and can make awards of up to £100,000. Always make sure that you follow the correct procedure or you could find that the Ombudsman cannot take up your case.

These are the financial ombudsmen:

■ Building Societies Ombudsman (0171 931 0044)

■ Pensions Ombudsman (0171 834 9144)

■ PIA (Personal Investment Authority) Ombudsman (0171 216 0016)

■ Insurance Ombudsman (0171 928 7600)

■ Investment Ombudsman (0171 796 3065)

■ Occupational Pensions Advisory Service (OPAS) (0171 233 8080)

Arbitration and Conciliation

If you deal with a company that is a member of a trade or professional body, that organization may offer an arbitration scheme or a conciliation service. Conciliation involves bringing both sides to an acceptable compromise. Arbitration is usually run by the Chartered Institute of Arbitrators, which runs a range of schemes with the independent arbitrators making a ruling (usually from documentation presented) and without a hearing.

Before pursing this route check the terms of the scheme. In some cases a ruling may not be binding on a member, or the member may refuse to go to arbitration or agree to conciliation. Be aware that some arbitration schemes are legally binding so that if you are not happy with the arbitrator's decision you may find that you cannot go to court afterwards. A small registration fee must usually be paid.

There are some industry wide arbitration schemes:

▓ Personal Insurance Arbitration Service (at the Chartered Institute of Arbitrators on 0171 837 4483)

▓ The Inland Revenue Adjudicator (ask you tax office for information on how to complain) or telephone 0171 930 2292

Small Claims Court

If you are seeking compensation or claiming £3000 or less (£1000 for personal injury cases), you can cut your legal costs by using the small claims court. In Scotland the limit is £750 and in Northern Ireland it is £1000.

This arbitration procedure is informal and proceedings are not heard in open court. You do not need a lawyer and you will have to pay a fee of only £10 to £80 depending on the amount of your claim. If you lose you may have to pay the other side's expenses for attending the hearing.

12 *Wills*

You may think you are far too young to worry about a will. But the consequences of failing to write one can be devastating. Your estranged parents, or brothers and sisters you never speak to can receive all your estate. And if you have no living relatives the Government will get everything.

Drawing up a will is essential, particularly if you are cohabiting as your partner has no legal rights to your estate if you die without making a will. (See joint ownership in Chapter 8 for more information). If you are married the rules of intestacy (if you fail to make a will) specify that your inheritance is split between your surviving spouse and children. If you are not married and have no children, other relatives will then inherit your estate. The rules vary depending on whether you come under English, Scottish or Northern Irish rules.

You can either buy a will-writing pack and draw up your own will or approach a solicitor, bank, building society, life insurance company or a specialist will-writing company.

Even if you seek professional advice in drawing up a will, you must make sure that it is drawn up correctly and that it meets your wishes. A recent *Which? Magazine* survey found that 15 out of 51 wills were poorly drawn up, and in some cases those designed to inherit may not have been able to because of confusing wording.

You will also need to appoint one or two executors who will administer your will on behalf of the beneficiaries. Be wary of appointing a professional executor at the time of will writing, as some banks and solicitors can charge high fees for dealing with probate.

Once you have drawn up a will you should review it regularly so that it reflects any changes in your circumstances. Finally, store your will in a safe place – preferably with a third party – where it can be easily found by your executors.

Index

Index of Advertisers